VISIONS *of* SOUTH TEXAS

Beyond the Ranch Gate

The Valley Land Fund Wildlife Photo Contest VI

Front Cover: Roseate Spoonbill
                   Photographer: Rex Hewitt
                   Landowner: Buena Vista Ranch

Back Cover: Rio Grande Leopard Frog
                   Photographer: Derrick Hamrick
                   Landowner: Las Colmenas Ranch

First Printing, 2005
Text and Photography Copyright© 2005 The Valley Land Fund

ISBN 0-9710604-2-8

Published by The Valley Land Fund

The Valley Land Fund
2400 North 10th Street, Suite A
McAllen, Texas 78501
www.valleylandfund.com

Wildlife Photo Contest
Phone: (956) 686-6429
Fax: (956) 686-1909
Email: contest@valleylandfund.com

Land Trust
Phone: (956) 971-8550
Fax: (956) 971-8565
Email: info@valleylandfund.com

Editor: Audrey Gluck Martin
Copy Editor: Jan Epton Seale
Contributing Editor: Lowry McAllen
Printing coordination and color: Bob Carter, Blue Fusion Design, Boulder, Colorado
Book and cover design: Esperanza S. Chapa, CopyZone, McAllen, Texas
Printing: Gateway Printing & Office Supply, Inc., Edinburg, Texas

Printed in the U.S.A.

Dedicated to Frank and Mary Yturria

Wildlife needs the help and support of all landowners to survive and thrive. Without participation by private landowners, wildlife conservation would be limited to public lands. In Texas, and South Texas specifically, public land comprises a very small fraction of critical wildlife habitat. Therefore, wildlife conservation in Texas depends primarily upon the commitment and stewardship of private landowners.

But private ownership of wildlife habitat does not guarantee a place for the unique plants and animals of South Texas. Some landowners would shoot a coyote rather than hear its howl. Others would bulldoze Granjeno or a Wild Olive for cropland instead of preserving the natural shelter and sustenance for native wildlife. Leadership by and education of private landowners about the benefits of wildlife conservation is the key to favorable results.

Frank and Mary Yturria have given invaluable time, energy, and resources to conserving and protecting South Texas wildlife. Stewards of a family ranching heritage that spans six generations, the Yturrias were founding members of The Valley Land Fund, which was established to educate private landowners and to foster wildlife conservation in South Texas. Their tireless and perennial efforts to support The Valley Land Fund and other conservation efforts in South Texas have proven effective and fruitful.

Frank and Mary granted conservation easements to the U.S. Fish and Wildlife Service to protect the endangered Ocelot. They donated land on the Laguna Madre to preserve marine habitat and have conveyed land to the Lower Rio Grande Valley National Wildlife Refuge. The Yturrias have also supported programs to protect the Texas Tortoise and the endangered Aplomado Falcon.

The Valley Land Fund proudly dedicates this book to Frank and Mary Yturria for their contributions to our wildlife, culture and community. They are an inspiration to us all–and from my point of view, a good cowman, an elegant woman and cherished family friends of admirable conscience.

–Tommy Lee Jones

About *Visions of South Texas*

Photographers from far and wide converged on the eight counties of the southern tip of Texas for the 2004 Valley Land Fund Wildlife Photo Contest. They produced thousands of pictures, but the prize-winning photographs are what make up this book. These images come from the South Texas Shootout, the Digital Competition, the Small Tract Competition and Youth Photo Contest–distinct competitions within the Wildlife Photo Contest.

This book, *Visions of South Texas: Beyond the Ranch Gate*, was produced by people from a variety of backgrounds and disciplines from throughout our community. Naturally, there were photographers and landowners, but this book was also made possible by writers, artists, naturalists and many other volunteers. And a number of steadfast and generous sponsors must be given credit for helping the book come into being.

Through them, and through you, the reader, The Valley Land Fund hopes to develop an important aspect of wildlife and habitat conservation: public awareness. Getting people to see and know our wildlife treasures is one of The Valley Land Fund's goals, and this is the organization's sixth book dedicated to that purpose.

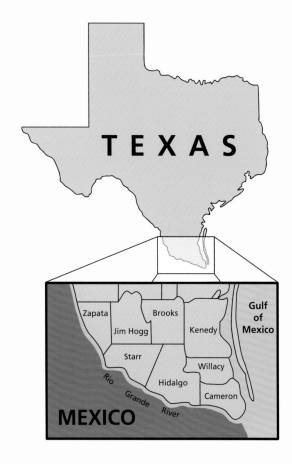

Table *of* Contents

Introduction

Go out into the early-morning darkness of our South Texas brush country. You might hear the lonely piping call of a Pauraque returning to roost from a night hunting insects. You might hear the rustling of Javelina bedding down before the heat of the day, and if they're near, you're sure to smell their musk. Just when the sun comes up, you'll observe a storm of birds starting their busy search for food. The Green Jays, Pyrrhuloxias and Mockingbirds declare that they are here long before they take their first bite. And you'll start to get a sense of just how lucky you are. Because you are in one of the most biologically diverse regions of the United States. By most counts, few other areas can keep up with us: birds, reptiles, butterflies, even mammals and plants. Think of all the biological treasures in the national parks of Yellowstone, the Everglades and Hawaii Volcanoes. The Lower Rio Grande Valley surpasses them all in the number of plant and animal species.

Two preserves in our area, Laguna Atascosa and Santa Ana, rank number one and number two for the greatest number of bird species in any national wildlife refuge. There are more butterflies in the eight counties covered by The Valley Land Fund contest than in all the states east of the Mississippi. And in our area, we have the longest stretch of undeveloped seacoast in the lower 48 states. There still remain wild tracts of land where the only man-made thing a Texas Tortoise on the ground would see is the occasional high-flying airplane, if that tortoise chose to lift its stoic head.

We sit at a unique junction in the natural world. In South Texas, the tropical meets the temperate. The Great Plains and the eastern forests meet the Chihuahuan Desert. The Rio Grande meets the Gulf of Mexico. Drawn into this cauldron of mixed landscapes and climates are thousands upon thousands of plants and animals, some that live here year round and others that come through in migration. Many of them simply cannot be found anywhere else in the United States.

So, during your morning walk through the brush, think of yourself as being in the capital of wild animal diversity. What New York is to finance and Hollywood is to film, South Texas is to wildlife. This is the kind of thing that makes a wildlife photographer's mouth water. Go through this book and you'll see why. Follow them as they use their talents to take you along on their own walk through the brush. Through their lens you catch a glimpse of what's out there. And what you see in this book is all on private land, which is still where the vast majority of South Texas native habitat thrives.

Private landowners set the stage for these images by opening their gates into the brush country. Their actions and this book are a testament to many things, not least of which is the responsibility that comes with owning land here. This is a wild land. And private landowners have helped keep it that way.

Some of the landowners that participated in The Valley Land Fund contest and the creation of this book are on land that their ancestors received as Spanish land grants, in a process that began as early as 1767. Yet these landowners and their predecessors have not wiped out our native habitat. They haven't plowed it under or poured asphalt across it or cleared it all with an ax. Their means for keeping the land together have been many. Some ranches have run profitable livestock operations. Some have used outside sources of income to hold it together when they didn't turn a profit. But by and large, they've done it because they were proud.

They were proud to be part of something this big and this wonderful. They were proud of the life and the ranches built by those who came before them. And these people have been determined that when they die they will leave the land for those who follow. This is a spirit of conservation that arose before anyone liked to use the word. And many newcomers have caught that spirit. They, too, have worked to keep the brush whole.

Keeping the land together and in brush, though, has been no small challenge. The Valley's population is one of the fastest growing in the country; in 30 years it has tripled. Great are the economic pressures to subdivide land into small parcels, which inevitably reduces native plants and wildlife. Time after time, the experts have found that cutting up habitat is the biggest threat to the survival of many plants and animals.

Take away one kind of living thing and others fall with it. Look at the Lyside Sulphur butterfly. Its food is one of our native plants, the Guayacán, one of the slowest growing in the Americas. How likely is that plant to survive the bulldozer and the plow? Hurt the Guayacán and you hurt the Lyside Sulphur. But this is only one example of the vital link between our special plants and animals and the soil and water

they live on. And it falls to us, those who value the miracles of the natural world, to do our best to keep it all together.

This can mean a lot of things, no matter whether you live on a large ranch or you live in town. From planting native plants to volunteer work to the donation of your resources, there's something you can do. The fact that you are holding this book in your hands shows that you're interested. And the brush, our native habitat, awaits you and your help.

So, at the end of your day, go back to that brush. Smell the lemon scent of a Colima bush or the vanilla of the Night Blooming Cereus cactus. Feel the heat loosen its grip. Listen for the creatures getting ready for the night ahead. All manner of crawling and climbing, flapping and fluttering will tickle your ear. And these signs of life ask us to let the brush blossom and flourish because of all the mystery it embodies, to let it be what it is, and let us always feel lucky and blessed that we should continue to be here with it.

Those sounds, and these pictures, are your invitation.

–Lowry McAllen

The Wildlife Photo Contest

Since its inception in 1994 and every other year thereafter, the Valley Land Fund's Wildlife Photo Contests have attracted landowners, photographers and sponsors to join their efforts in an amazing event.

In the contests, photographers with wide-ranging levels of skill and commitment, and using all manner of equipment and gear, set out on a scavenger hunt of sorts to capture images of as wide a variety of animals as possible.

Landowners and photographers form partnerships for these events, which not only pay prize money to the contestants, but also provide funds to be used for land conservation projects.

While encouraging landowners to conserve and enhance valuable wildlife habitat, the contests also opened venues for photographers to explore and push to the limit the art of wildlife photography. Cash prizes now totaling in excess of $500,000 have been awarded equally to both photographers and landowners, creating very real incentives for participating in the contest.

The contests have presently evolved to allow professional, amateur, and youth photographers access to private lands, including large ranches, small tracts, and even backyards. Youth photographers may even compete on some public lands in the Valley, except for zoos.

Though often not apparent in the photographs, much of the wildlife shown exists only because the landowners of large tracts have been historically committed to the land and its wildlife. Conversely, via the observant and imaginative eyes of the photographers, landowners have often rediscovered the abundant and rich diversity of the wildlife on their properties.

With the completion of this book, the two-year cycle of the contest has been fully repeated six times. Running the richest wildlife photography contest in the world requires literally thousands of hours of work by a small, dedicated staff and a large group of board members and other volunteers.

Immediately after the photo contest awards celebration, usually held the last weekend of August, work begins with the formation of new photo contest committees and scheduling of events for the next cycle. Budgets are established, sponsors are recruited, contest format is reviewed and modified, judges are selected, and brochures and entry forms are designed, printed and distributed. Landowners and photographers sign up and entry forms and fees are received. In addition to the entry fees, financial support from generous sponsors becomes the lifeblood of the contest.

At the conclusion of each of the previous six contests, and running concurrently with the planning and implementation of each new photo contest, the rather complicated process of designing, producing, editing and publishing a book has occurred. Carefully, and creatively crafted using photographs and words, the book becomes an artful, educational, and persuasive tool. Enjoyable and instructive to all, it inspires interest in future contests as well as involvement in The Valley Land Fund's mission.

Through the educational spirit of all of the previous contests and books, the VLF has raised awareness of the value in conserving, protecting and sometimes creating wildlife habitat.

–Bob Simpson

Foreword

Wildlife photography will show you things you never knew existed. It will reveal scenes that are beyond your own experience and sometimes beyond your imagination.

Take the examples you are about to see in this book. There's an adult Mockingbird feeding an orange berry to its young. Now ask yourself when the last time was that you saw a mockingbird with its baby.

Look at another image in this book, of Red Velvet Mites, those strange arachnids that are fluffy and crimson red and aren't so easy to find. Have you ever seen them? They come out in the sun just after a rain, usually on those days when it's cool but not too cold.

These pictures will tell you something else about wildlife photography: looking at the images is the easy part. Their creators, the photographers who were in The Valley Land Fund contest, spent thousands of hours in the field. They waited and they waited, hardly moving, sometimes trying to quiet the sounds of their own breath until the right moment happened.

What they reveal for us is amazing, but the beauty in these pictures goes far beyond the color and the habits of these animals. You see, these creatures are with us every day, every second, thriving in the wild. They are around us all the time, but how many of us would see them without the eyes of these photographers?

–Nolan Ryan

South Texas Shootout

Amidst diverse habitat and abundant wildlife, landowners and photographers combined in the lush springtime and early summer of 2004 to compete in the sixth South Texas Shootout. Likened to a treasure hunt, the photographers, sometimes pairing in teams of two, worked with landowners, also sometimes in twosomes, to try to find and photograph wildlife species from 50 classes. The goal of this treasure hunt was to capture on film the most unique and beautiful images of wildlife that South Texas has to offer.

Photographers each submitted portfolios of up to one hundred 35mm slides for judging by three highly respected judges. The judges individually scored the submissions, awarding points to each image, with bonus points given to those images selected for the top three places in each class. Additional bonus points were awarded to those images selected for the top three places in each of five divisions: Birds, Mammals, Insects & Arachnids, Reptiles & Amphibians and Special Categories, including Action, Animal Babies, Camouflage, Humor, Landscape/Waterscape, Patterns, and Sunrise/Sunset. The top five overall point recipients were designated Grand Prize Winners. A total of 30 landowner/photographer teams won cash prizes totaling $130,000, making this the world's richest wildlife photo contest.

Judges also selected the individual photo that they thought was "Best of Contest" while the "People's Choice" was selected by popular vote at the El Monte awards ceremony.

–Bob Simpson

South Texas Shootout
GRAND PRIZE PORTFOLIOS
TOP *five* WINNERS

First Grand Prize

Photographer: Rolf Nussbaumer

Landowners: Phil and Karen Hunke / Cleve and Rosemary Breedlove
El Tecolote Ranch / Inn at Chachalaca Bend

Rolf Nussbaumer
Photo by Karen Nussbaumer

Karen and Phil Hunke
Photo by Bob Simpson

Cleve and Rosemary Breedlove

The South Texas Shootout, so demanding that it is held only every other year, is considered the "Iron Man" of wildlife photo contests. No one had ever won it twice until Rolf Nussbaumer, a native of Switzerland, accomplished the feat by garnering the grand prize in 2002 and 2004.

Beginning on February 1 and running through June 30, the contest focused on each photographer's total portfolio and stipulated a maximum of 100 shots from five distinct wildlife divisions. "It was a really hard five months, but I think the key for me was persistence," Nussbaumer said.

Nussbaumer, who now resides in San Antonio, divided his time between two very different properties. He spent approximately two thirds of his time on Phil and Karen Hunke's ranch in northern Hidalgo County, and the remaining third on Cleve and Rosemary Breedlove's property in eastern Cameron County.

"It would obviously be very difficult for anyone to win just on this property, as we don't have the large mammals," Cleve Breedlove explained. The Breedloves live on 40 acres of pristine riparian resaca woodlands near Los Fresnos. The Inn at Chachalaca Bend is prime habitat for a marvelous variety of tropical birds such as Buff-bellied Hummingbirds and Chachalacas.

"No one had ever won with a Chachalaca," Rosemary noted, "and we so hoped Rolf would get a winning shot and he did."

Cleve added, "It is great having a talented photographer on your property, because they find so many things you just didn't know you had."

Nussbaumer took full advantage of Karen and Phil Hunke's brush country wildlands and photographed a variety of creatures, from secretive Ferruginous Pygmy-Owls to colorful Caracaras.

"Having a photographer like Rolf on our ranch was a wonderful, exciting experience," Karen said. "It is sort of like a treasure hunt, and you learn so much about what you really have on your land."

Phil observed, "We knew it was a privilege to be able to buy the ranch, and we have always managed the property with habitat as our first priority."

The Hunkes and Breedloves are both planning to enter their land once again in the 2006 contest. And if you ask Rolf Nussbaumer if he is contemplating a "triple crown," he just laughs and says, "I might enter again, I really don't know. I do enjoy sharing my photographs with other people."

–Richard Moore

The Buff-bellied Hummingbird is a jewel among birds. Sunlight reflecting off its green throat shimmers as the tiny hummer feeds from its favorite native plant, the Hammond's Turks Cap. The "buffy" is the only "hummer" that stays year-round in South Texas, although a good number migrate south.

Nikon F5 with 300mm f2.8 AF lens and extension tube; 1/250 sec at f22; Fuji Sensia 100

Buff-bellied Hummingbird

FIRST PLACE, Hummingbirds, Nightjars, Swallows and Swifts
THIRD PLACE, Birds Division

Savannah Sparrow
SECOND PLACE, Sparrows & Towhees

During the winter months in South Texas the countryside experiences a dramatic increase in sparrows of many species. The most numerous is the Savannah Sparrow, which can be found by the hundreds in fields, pastures, and fence rows.

Nikon F5 with 600mm f4 AF 1 lens and teleconverter; 1/320 sec at f8; Fuji Sensia 100

Green Jay
SECOND PLACE, Blackbirds, Jays, Orioles, Tanagers

The Green Jay makes its home only in South Texas and further south, and is part of the Corvid family, which includes crows and similar birds. They are raucous and gregarious, often coming to backyard feeders and chasing off other songbirds.

Nikon F5 with 600mm f4 AF 1 lens and teleconverter; 1/250 sec at f8; Fuji Sensia 100

Raccoon

FIRST PLACE, Mustelids & Raccoons

This masked bandit is mostly nocturnal but can be seen during the day at times. Found mainly near ponds and other waterways, the opportunistic Raccoon will feed on fruits, nuts, grains, insects, frogs and more.

Nikon F5 with 300mm f2.8 AF lens; 1/125 sec at f8; Kodak E100VS

White-tipped Dove

FIRST PLACE, Doves, Parakeets,
Parrots, Pigeons

A parent's job is never done, even for the White-tipped Dove, which may choose to nest in a Prickly Pear Cactus. This large and distinct dove is not found any further north than South Texas, where it is mostly seen walking on the ground in heavy brush.

Nikon F5 with 600mm f4 1 lens; 1/80 sec at f5.6; Fuji Sensia 100

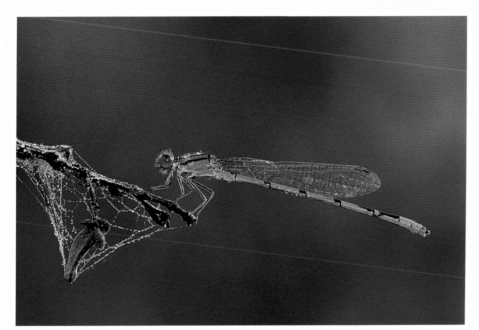

Familiar Bluet
SECOND PLACE, Damselflies & Dragonflies

Damselflies such as the Familiar Bluet are closely related to the dragonfly but can be distinguished from them because damselflies fold their wings over their back. "Damsels" can be found in areas with moist tall grass.

Nikon F5 with 200mm f4 micro lens; 1/60 sec at f11; Kodak E100VS

Belted Kingfisher
THIRD PLACE, All Other Birds

This master fisher dives underwater to catch its prey. Unlike most bird species, the male shows a less colorful plumage than the female, which sports a rusty band across her belly.

Nikon F5 with 600mm f4 AF 1 lens and teleconverter; 1/400 sec at f8; Fuji Provia 100

Bewick's Wren

FIRST PLACE, Gnatcatchers, Kinglets, Nuthatches, Titmice, Verdins, Vireos, Warblers, Wrens

A tiny bird with a big voice, the Bewick's Wren is often heard but seldom seen, as it stays hidden in dense vegetation, scolding any intruder with its raucous calls.

Nikon F5 with 300mm f2.8 AF 1 lens and extension tube; 1/250 sec at f22; Fuji Sensia 100

Least Grebe

SECOND PLACE, Animal Babies

The colorful youngsters of a Least Grebe stand in contrast to their plain-plumaged parents. These juvenile birds catch a free ride while staying protected on Mom's back.

Nikon F5 with 600mm f4 AF 1 lens and teleconverter; 1/320 sec at f8; Fuji Sensia 100

Common Pauraque

THIRD PLACE, Hummingbirds, Nightjars, Swallows, Swifts

A true master of camouflage, the Common Pauraque may be overlooked
as it roosts on the ground during daylight hours. This bird consumes huge numbers of mosquitoes each night and can be seen sitting on country roads before dawn, its eyes reflecting red in the headlights.

Nikon F5 with 600mm f4 AF 1 lens and extension tube; 1/250 sec at f8; Kodak E100VS

Chestnut-sided Warbler

THIRD PLACE, Gnatcatchers, Kinglets, Nuthatches, Titmice, Verdins, Vireos, Warblers, Wrens

The wood warblers are a family distinct to the New World. They often display brilliant plumage and are known for their rapid movement as they feed. The Chestnut-sided Warbler is easily distinguished by its yellow-green and chestnut-colored sides.

Nikon F5 with 600mm f4 AF 1 lens and extension tube; 1/60 sec at f8; Fuji Sensia 100

Whirlabout

SECOND PLACE, Butterflies I

Grass skippers such as the Whirlabout are sometimes considered to be the "sparrows" of the butterfly world. They can be very similar to each other in coloration and hard to tell apart. The Whirlabout gets its name from its habit of landing and taking off in a circular flight.

Nikon F5 with 200mm f4 micro lens; 1/15 sec at f16; Kodak E100VS

Colorful beetles are a common sight on various blooming flowers. The Blister Beetle is aptly named for the uncomfortable blisters that it may produce on humans.

Nikon F5 with 200mm f4 micro lens; 1/250 sec at f16; Fuji Velvia

Blister Beetle
FIRST PLACE, Beetles

Little Yellow

FIRST PLACE, Butterflies II
SECOND PLACE, Insects & Arachnids Division

The Little Yellow is aptly named. The beautiful Plains Coreopsis flower is a wonderful source of nectar.

Nikon F5 with 200mm f4 AF micro lens; 1/15 sec at f16; Fuji Velvia

Sphinx Moth

FIRST PLACE, Moths

The Sphinx Moth hovers in front of flowers and feeds on nectar with its very long "tongue," leading it to be called the Hummingbird Moth. It has a clear white stripe across its lower body, which gives away its true moth identity.

Nikon F5 with 200mm f4 AF micro lens; 1/250 sec at f11; Fuji Sensia 100

Jumping Spider

THIRD PLACE, Spiders

By far the most advanced spider, this boldly patterned creature has superior eyesight and an inquisitive nature. It can leap great distances away from a perceived threat.

Nikon F5 with 200mm f4 AF micro lens and extension tubes; 1/30 sec at f16; Kodak E100VS

Ferruginous Pygmy-Owl

THIRD PLACE, Birds of Prey II

Pound for pound this little owl is an aggressive predator, daily eating its weight in lizards, insects and other small creatures. Frequently a day hunter, it is sometimes mobbed by song birds.

Nikon F5 with 600 f4 AF 1 lens; 1/250 sec at f8; Fuji Sensia 100

Praying Mantis
FIRST PLACE, All Other Insects

Named for its forelegs held as if praying, this insect is one fierce predator. The Praying Mantis is an expert hunter and has even been known to catch hummingbirds.

Nikon F5 with 200mm f4 AF micro lens; 1/200 sec at f11; Kodak E100VS

Checkered Garter Snake

FIRST PLACE, Non-venomous Snakes I

Checkered Garter Snakes can be seen around bodies of water where they feed on small fish and frogs. Sometimes found wandering across land at night after summer rains, they emit a foul-smelling musk as a defense if picked up.

Nikon F5 with 200mm f4 AF micro lens; 1/100 sec at f16; Fuji Velvia

Crested Caracara

SECOND PLACE, Birds of Prey I

This bird assumes a stately pose in grassy pastures, surveying its surroundings.
Caracaras may be found along roadsides as they wait for a meal.

Nikon F5 with 600mm f4 AF 1 lens; 1/400 sec at f/8; Fuji Sensia 100

Plain Chachalaca

SECOND PLACE, Chachalacas, Quail, Turkeys

Greeting the early day with a chorus of loud calls, the male Plain Chachalaca is recognized
by its red throat pouch. A rather secretive bird in the wild, it has adapted well
to residential neighborhoods, where it has lost its shyness
and readily comes to feeders and baths.

Nikon F5 with 600mm f4 AF 1 lens and teleconverter; 1/320 sec at f8; Fuji Sensia 100

Barn Owl
SECOND PLACE, Birds of Prey II

The "ghost of the night" may roost in old barns during the day, thus the name Barn Owl. This owl is a wonderful mouser, bringing in rodent after rodent to hungry chicks.

Nikon F5 with 20mm f2.8 lens; 45 min at f16; Fuji Sensia 100

True Bug
SECOND PLACE, All Other Insects

True Bugs can be found throughout South Texas. Immature insects can be determined by their "wing buds" that will eventually become wings.

Nikon F5 with 200mm f4 AF micro lens; 1/8 sec at f16; Kodak E100VS

Northern Cardinal

FIRST PLACE, Buntings, Cardinals, Grosbeaks, Pyrrhuloxias

The redbird, as it was known of old, benefits from an occasional bath. The Northern Cardinal is not known for being a backyard feeding species in South Texas but is numerous in the brush country. The male's bright red color is a true showstopper.

Nikon F5 with 600m f4 AF 1 lens and extension tube and teleconverter; 1/200 sec at f18; Fuji Sensia 100

Mediterranean Gecko

SECOND PLACE, All Other Reptiles

Mediterranean Geckos can climb vertical walls with the tiny velcro-like hooks present under their toes. They lack eyelids and clean their lenses with their tongue.

Nikon F5 with 200 f4 AF micro lens; 1/250 sec at f16; Kodak E100VS

Paper Wasp

THIRD PLACE, Ants, Bees, Wasps

The paper wasp, often labeled as aggressive, only attacks if disturbed. This very common wasp may build its nest under eaves of homes, but it prefers the undersides of native Sabal Palm tree leaves.

Nikon F5 with 200mm f4 AF micro lens; 1/125 sec at f16; Kodak E100VS

This bird makes an unusual link in the food chain. The Laughing Gull's been known to swoop down and pluck fish from the gaping mouths of pelicans. But this gull is sometimes forced to give up its meals to roguish Frigatebirds and Jaegers.

Nikon F5 with 600mm f4 AF 1 lens; 1/800 sec at f5.6; Fuji Sensia 100

Laughing Gull
FIRST PLACE, Water Birds II

Thornbush Dasher

THIRD PLACE, Damselflies & Dragonflies

Dragonflies are fierce predators despite their small size and can eat thousands of mosquitoes, making them our friend. Often found around water holes, some such as the Thornbush Dasher prefer drier habitats.

Nikon F5 with 200mm f4 AF micro lens; 1/8 sec at f11; Kodak E100VS

Gulf Coast Ribbon Snake

SECOND PLACE, Non-venomous Snakes

Gulf Coast Ribbon Snakes are common around ponds and resacas where they feed on fish, frogs and tadpoles. Congregations occur during the spring breeding season.

Nikon F5 with 200mm f4 AF micro lens; 1/250 sec at f22; Fuji Sensia 100

White-striped Longtail

FIRST PLACE, Butterflies I

Stopping for a meal of nectar, the White-striped Longtail finds a Plains Coreopsis flower to its liking. This butterfly is only found in South Texas and Mexico, where it uses viney legumes as its host plant.

Nikon F5 with 200mm f4 AF micro lens; 1/30 sec at f11; Fuji Velvia

Mexican Tree Frog

SECOND PLACE, Frogs & Toads
SECOND PLACE, Reptiles and Amphibians Division

The Mexican Tree Frog, common in Mexico, can be found as far north as the southernmost tip of Texas. The male makes his call with a double vocal pouch.

Nikon F5 with 200mm f4 AF micro lens; 1/15 sec at f16; Kodak E100VS

Buff-bellied Hummingbird

THIRD PLACE, Action

A favorite of many who enjoy nature's bounty is the small but feisty Buff-bellied Hummingbird. Known for consuming large quantities of nectar, its diet also includes small insects caught in mid-flight.

Nikon F5 with 300mm f2.8 AF 1 lens and extension tube; 1/250 sec at f22; Fuji Sensia 100

The well-camouflaged Eastern Screech-Owl stalks its prey near dusk and dawn. Its soft feathers allow for silent flight, and it can surprise any creature venturing out at night, sometimes even taking prey heavier than its own body weight.

Nikon F5 with 24-50mm f4.5 AF lens; 1/250 sec at f11; Fuji Sensia 100

Eastern Screech-Owl
FIRST PLACE, Birds of Prey II

Pied-billed Grebe

THIRD PLACE, Water Birds I

"Pied" means splotchy or striped in Middle English. This diving bird frequents both fresh and brackish waters and is commonly seen as it tends to its young.

Nikon F5 with 600mm f4 AF 1 lens; 1/320 sec at f8; Fuji Sensia 100

Moth Caterpillar

SECOND PLACE, Moths

Moving its way across the plant in a peculiar fashion, this moth caterpillar is often referred to as the "Inch Worm."

Nikon F5 with 200mm f4 AF micro lens and extension tube; 1/8 sec at f22; Fuji Velvia

Brown-crested Flycatcher

FIRST PLACE, Flycatchers & Kingbirds

Flycatching from a high tree branch for large insects is the main food-gathering technique of the Brown-crested Flycatcher. It arrives in South Texas in late spring and spends the summer raising its young.

Nikon F5 with 600mm f4 AF 1 lens; 1/320 sec. at f8; Kodak E100VS

Celia's Roadside-Skippers

THIRD PLACE, Butterflies I

Nature is intricate in design, and a good example is the relationship between butterflies, such as these Celia's Roadside-Skippers and the plants on which they lay their eggs. Many butterflies use very few species of plants on which to rear their young.

Nikon F5 with 200mm f4 micro lens; 1/15 sec at f16; Fuji Sensia 100

Nature does nothing uselessly.

–Aristotle

Second Grand Prize

Photographer: Derrick Hamrick

Landowner: Robert & Margaret McAllen
Las Colmenas Ranch

Derrick Hamrick

The ranch covers some 4,500 acres of grassland and native habitat in northwestern Hidalgo County, and the family can trace the ranch's history back to the 1791 land grant of an ancestor.

It's a working cattle ranch, and Lowry and Jessica McAllen are the only full-time hands. Hunting provides some added income but the living is not easy. Now these pioneers are breaking ground in nature tourism, with the day-leasing of specially designed photo areas to wildlife photographers.

(L-R) Margaret, Robert, Jessica and Lowry McAllen
Photo by Audrey G. Martin

The McAllens have a deep-seated respect for the land and a conservation ethic passed from parents to son. Some of the rotational grazing practices that sustain the ranch were gleaned from information on herd animals in Africa. As a result, both cattle and wildlife flourish in this harsh yet diverse and resilient land.

Robert and Margaret McAllen turned over management in 2002 to their son Lowry when he and his bride Jessica came to live at the ranch. Lowry holds a degree in anthropology and has seven years' experience as a journalist, while Jessica has a liberal arts degree and hails from New York City. What prepared them to run the ranch? "Critical thinking," says Lowry.

Las Colmenas has been in every VLF contest since the competition's inception in 1994. Robert says he "just wanted to participate in a project that sounded awfully good." Margaret adds, "We're Valley natives; we love the area and wanted to learn more about our land."

They all agree that the photo contest has helped to create an awareness of the richness of habitat but believe that the resulting book is the real conservation tool, since it brings the wildlife out for others to see.

Derrick Hamrick spent five long months on Las Colmenas, waking at daybreak, with grueling days in the heat, trying any trick imaginable for that special shot. A retired fireman from Raleigh, North Carolina, Derrick is known as an "extreme photographer" who will do anything for a shot as long as it doesn't jeopardize the subject.

After finding Jaguarundi tracks around a water hole, Derrick dug a small bunker and outfitted it for a ten-day stay, planning to be there day and night until he could photograph this rare and elusive cat. The cat never showed and a torrential rain flooded him out after four days.

This was his third VLF contest. He is in awe of the variety of wildlife in South Texas and says he's also learned that you can step within two feet of a rattlesnake and *sometimes* not get struck!

–Audrey G. Martin

Rio Grande Leopard Frog

FIRST PLACE, Frogs & Toads
FIRST PLACE, Reptiles & Amphibians Division

The Rio Grande Leopard Frog occurs in large numbers in stock tanks on South Texas ranches. It is an important source of food for raccoons, snakes, turtles, herons and many other species.

Canon 1 NRS with 400mm lens; 1/250 sec at f22; Kodak Elite 100

Mediterranean Gecko

THIRD PLACE, All Other Reptiles

Mediterranean Geckos are nocturnal and are frequently seen around porch lights and window screens. Their bellies are transparent and eggs can be seen inside gestating females. The eggs are laid behind walls, picture frames, stacked pots and other structures or debris.

Canon EOS 3 with 180mm macro lens; 1/2 sec at f16; Kodak Elite 100

Mourning Dove

SECOND PLACE, Doves, Parakeets, Parrots, Pigeons

The Mourning Dove was given its name because of the mournful calls it makes and not from the "morning," as is often thought. One of several migratory game birds, this abundant dove is found throughout North America.

Canon EOS 3 with 400mm 2.8 IS lens and 2x teleconverter; 1/250 sec at f8; Kodak Elite 100

White-tailed Deer

FIRST PLACE, White-tailed Deer
SECOND PLACE, Mammals Division

White-tailed Deer are shy inhabitants of the ranch lands of South Texas,
where they can best be seen near their favorite watering hole.
Their large antlers, which regrow each year,
are initially covered in "velvet."

Canon EOS 3 with 400mm 2.8mm IS lens; 1/125 sec at f8; Kodak Elite 100

Familiar Bluet

FIRST PLACE, Damselflies & Dragonflies
FIRST PLACE, Insects & Arachnids Division

The Familiar Bluet belongs to the narrow-winged damselfly family. This female damselfly is just an example of the many wonderful discoveries to be made outdoors.

Canon EOS 3 with 180mm macro lens; 1/2 sec at f22; Kodak Elite 100

Dickcissel

SECOND PLACE, Action

Migrating birds use the South Texas landscape as a stopover and refueling station. Dickcissel migration is currently under study, with monitoring stations at some local high schools in South Texas.

Canon EOS 3 with 400mm 2.8 IS lens and 2x teleconverter; 1/500 sec at f8; Kodak Elite 100

White-tipped Dove

THIRD PLACE, Doves, Parakeets, Parrots, Pigeons

A bird overlooked due to its ability to blend in with its surroundings, the White-tipped Dove is actually a rather splendid dove when seen up close.

Canon EOS 3 with 400mm 2.8 IS lens and 2x teleconverter; 1/125 sec at f8; Kodak Elite 100

Eastern Cottontail

THIRD PLACE, Rabbits & Hares

Water is one of the most important elements in the daily life of wild animals. After a long hot South Texas day, the Eastern Cottontail is one of many that seek out watering holes in the cooler evening hours.

Canon EOS 3 with 400mm 2.8 IS lens; 1/125 sec at f8; Kodak Elite 100

Least Grebe

SECOND PLACE, Water Birds I

Transporting its young safely tucked on its back, the Least Grebe inhabits small quiet freshwater ponds. Its intensely orange eyes are always watching the surroundings for danger.

Canon EOS 3 with 400 mm 2.8 IS lens and 2x teleconverter; 1/125 sec at f8; Kodak Elite 100

Living a nocturnal life, the Virginia Opossum is found in most South Texas habitats as well as in suburban areas. Its somewhat scruffy looks and habits have not earned it an endearing spot with most people. The Opossum is best known for its ability to play dead when threatened.

Canon EOS 3 with 17-35mm lens; 1/200 sec at f8; Kodak Elite 100

Virginia Opossum
FIRST PLACE, All Other Mammals

Raccoon

THIRD PLACE, Mustelids & Raccoons

Adorable as it appears, the Raccoon is a master at trickery and can find its way into all sorts of trouble, including hen houses, storage sheds and trash cans. Favorite habitats include woods with a nearby water source.

Canon EOS 3 with 400mm 2.8 IS lens; 1/125 sec at f5.6; Kodak Elite 100

Moth Caterpillar

THIRD PLACE, Moths

Moth caterpillars are often striking in beauty and comprise several colorful groups, including the Tiger Moth family. They may be clothed in stiff-haired attire to fend off predators, and many roll up in little rings when threatened.

Canon EOS 3 with 180mm macro lens; 1/2 sec at f16; Kodak Elite 100

The imported Honey Bee has slowly been giving way to the Africanized Bee in South Texas. Bees not only add color and beauty to the landscape, they also perform the very important task of pollinating native flower species.

Canon EOS 3 with 90mm lens and 2x teleconverter; 1/4 sec at f32; Kodak Elite 100

Honey Bee

FIRST PLACE, Ants, Bees, Wasps & Other Insects
THIRD PLACE, Insects & Arachnids Division

Barn Owl
FIRST PLACE, Humor

Owls have been associated with much folklore involving wisdom and death. Baby Barn Owls, however, have a knack for creating smiles and laughs with their clumsy antics and comical appearance.

Canon EOS 3 with 17-35mm lens; 1/200 sec at f16; Kodak Elite 100

Emarginea percara

SECOND PLACE, Camouflage

Moths are masters of disguise, blending with their surroundings to the point of disappearing. Can you find the moth on the lichen-covered tree?
Many moths have no common names, such as the *Emarginea percara*, which is referred to by its Latin name.

Canon EOS 3 with 180mm macro lens; 1/30 sec at f22; Kodak Elite 100

Northern Cat-eyed Snake

SECOND PLACE, Venomous Snakes

The Northern Cat-eyed Snake is one of the rarest snakes of South Texas. It has rear fangs used to subdue its prey of frogs and lizards. Nocturnal, its elliptical pupils expand at night when it searches for prey around ponds and other small bodies of water.

Canon EOS 3 with 180mm macro lens; 1/200 sec at f16; Kodak Elite 100

Barn Owl

THIRD PLACE, Humor

With faces only a mother could love, the Barn Owl's young can be a laughable lot. When cold, they huddle together for warmth and protection.

Canon EOS 3 with 17-35mm lens; 1/200 sec at f16; Kodak Elite 100

Longhorn Grasshopper

THIRD PLACE, All Other Insects

Much like reptiles shed their skins, so do some insects. The antennae that adorn the Longhorn family of grasshoppers resemble the horns of our famous Texas cattle.

Canon EOS 3 with 100-400mm 5.6 zoom lens; 1/4 sec at f11; Kodak Elite 100

So many creatures that inhabit the South Texas chaparral are never seen. The Striped Scorpion lives in cracks and crevices in many types of habitats and is the most common scorpion. While painful, its sting is not serious to humans, but certainly would be fatal to freeloading moths.

Canon EOS 3 with 180mm macro lens; 1/200 sec at f22; Kodak Elite 100

Striped Scorpion
FIRST PLACE, All Other Arachnids

Wild Turkey

FIRST PLACE, Patterns
FIRST PLACE, Special Categories Division

As if painted by a master, the patterns adorning the feathers of the Wild Turkey are spectacular to behold. Commonly associated with the holiday of Thanksgiving, this bird can be found year round in the South Texas brush country.

Canon EOS with 90mm lens; 1/15 sec at f32; Kodak Elite 100

Leaf Beetle

THIRD PLACE, Beetles

These small beetles start their life cycle underground and only the adults are seen feeding on leafy plants. Hundreds of species of Leaf Beetles occur in North America.

Canon EOS 3 with 180mm macro lens; Kodak Elite 100

Land Snail

THIRD PLACE, All Other Arthropods & Snails

Often found on Prickly Pear Cactus or other South Texas scrub brush, the Land Snail is favorite food for the rare Hook-billed Kite. It is said that rain is coming soon if the snails venture high into the vegetation.

Canon EOS 3 with 180mm macro lens; 1/15 sec at f8; Kodak Elite 100

Plains Black-headed Snake

THIRD PLACE, Non-venomous Snakes I

The Plains Black-headed Snake is a small secretive burrowing species. One component of its diet is centipedes, which are subdued with a mild venom delivered by enlarged rear teeth. Black-headed Snakes are not aggressive. They rarely bite when handled, and their venom is harmless to humans.

Canon EOS 3 with 180mm macro lens; 1/200 sec at f8; Kodak Elite 100

Nature and books belong to the eyes that see them.

–Ralph Waldo Emerson

Third Grand Prize

Photographer: **Bill Draker**

Landowner: **Tecomate Ranch Partners**

Bill Draker is a bona fide Texan who lives on a 500-acre cattle ranch in the Hill Country between Bandera and Kerrville. He spent some of his youth visiting a ranch in South Texas, where he came to love this land we call home. What stands out in Bill's mind, in contrasting these two areas of the state, is the abundance of wildlife in South Texas, especially the birds. You can hear the excitement in his voice as he talks about the many Cardinals he has seen in the Rio Grande Valley.

In his youth, Bill hunted in the wild but, as he says, "It takes more skill to shoot a deer with a camera than with a gun, and the camera can 'shoot' that deer many times." Bill first took an interest in photography in the early 1970s during a trip to Alaska. He used an Instamatic camera, and, to be amply supplied, took along only three rolls of film! Once the film was developed, Bill saw too many fingers and straps in the photos. He was convinced that he needed to upgrade. The 2004 contest was his fifth Valley Land Fund Wildlife Photo Contest.

In all five contests, Bill used the same land, the 10,000-acre Tecomate Ranch. Its owners, a diverse group including Dr. Gary M. Schwarz and Dr. Steve Shepard, have consistently demonstrated a commitment to land conservation while carrying on the values of the ranch's former owner, the V. H. Guerra family.

In the early years of the contest, there were no water features or blinds on the ranch. Bill photographed with a partner at that time, and together they piped in water and set up blinds that contributed to their always being among the top winners. For the last three contests, Bill entered individually. There's enough wildlife, he says, on the two acres around a pond and a house where he stays to keep him busy the entire six months of the contest. In his words, the contest is very demanding. The dryness and heat of South Texas make it tough. Spending a lot of time with the animals is a must. Just knowing how to use a camera isn't enough. One must know the animals and their habits.

This past contest, Bill wanted a picture of a family of grebes. A pair started coming to the water hole, and soon they built a nest. During the entire contest, that nest was destroyed, eggs and all, at least four times due to hail, wind and predators. Bill didn't get his picture, but those grebes gave him something better: on the last day of the contest, they were rebuilding that nest again. Never give up.

–Clare Bercot

The Least Grebe, the smallest North American Grebe, is found only in South Texas where it builds floating nests of reeds on small freshwater ponds.

Canon 1V with 500mm f4 IS lens and 2x teleconverter; 1/125 sec at f11; Fuji Sensia 100

Least Grebe

FIRST PLACE, Water Birds I
FIRST PLACE, Birds Division
BEST OF CONTEST

Northern Mockingbird

FIRST PLACE, Catbirds, Mockingbirds,
Shrikes, Thrashers, Thrushes

The state bird of Texas can out-talk any Texan. Mockers are excellent mimics who find ample nourishment in the brush country, feeding their young berries and insects.

Canon 1V with 500mm f4 IS lens and 1.4x teleconverter; 1/250 sec at f8; Fuji Sensia 100

Vermilion Flycatcher

THIRD PLACE, Animal Babies

Hungry mouths are a common sight during late spring and summer in the South Texas brush. Many species of birds nest throughout the region and add a special beauty to the landscape.

Canon 1V with 500mm f4 lens and 2x teleconverter; 1/250 sec at f8; Fuji Sensia 100

Anacamptodes dataria

THIRD PLACE, Camouflage

Camouflage is one of nature's ways to protect many animal species, which use colors and patterns to blend into their surroundings. Moths, such as the group referred to as Geometrids, are a wonderful example of this defense.

Canon 1V with 180mm macro lens; 1/250 sec at f16; Fuji Sensia 100

Texas Horned Lizard

SECOND PLACE, Anoles, Geckos, Lizards & Skinks

Texas Horned Lizards have disappeared over much of the state, but many areas of South Texas still have thriving populations. Red Harvester Ants are their main source of food. Both horned lizards and harvester ants should be protected by landowners.

Canon 1V with 180mm macro lens; 1/250 sec at f16; Fuji Sensia 100

Red-eared Slider

THIRD PLACE, Tortoises and Turtles

Red-eared Sliders are frequently seen basking on logs in bodies of water in South Texas. Females have short claws, but the long claws of the males are used in courtship for scratching the female on her face.

Canon 1V with 500mm f4 IS lens and 2x teleconverter; 1/250 sec at f8; Fuji Sensia 100

Spotted Ground Squirrel

SECOND PLACE, Humor

In South Texas the Spotted Ground Squirrel hides from the heat by resting in its burrow midday. It is primarily a vegetarian, but will dine on grasshoppers and beetles.

Canon 1V with 500mm f4 IS lens and 1.4x teleconverter; 1/125 sec at f11; Fuji Sensia 100

Greater Roadrunner

THIRD PLACE, Anis, Cuckoos, Roadrunners

Seen running along ranch roads in the South Texas brush country, the Greater Roadrunner does act like his cartoon counterpart. The roadrunner can be shy, at times hiding behind cactus, only heard by the low rattling sound produced by its bill.

Canon 1V with 500mm f4 IS lens and 2x teleconverter; 1/125 sec at f11; Fuji Sensia 100

Curve-billed Thrasher

THIRD PLACE, Catbirds, Mockingbirds, Shrikes, Thrashers, Thrushes

Scratching out a living in the leaf litter of woody thickets, the Curve-billed Thrasher finds tasty insects. Obviously named for its curved bill, it also sports bright orange eyes which contrast with its grayish plumage.

Canon 1V with 500mm f4 IS lens and 1.4x teleconverter; 1/125 sec at f11; Fuji Sensia 100

This we know: the earth does not belong to man, man belongs to the earth.
All things are connected like the blood that unites us all.
Man did not weave the web of life, he is merely a strand in it.
Whatever he does to the web, he does to himself.

–Seattle, Chief of the Squamish

Fourth Grand Prize

Photographer: **Larry Ditto**

Landowner: **Roel Ramírez**

Ramírez Ranch

Roel Ramírez was born in Rio Grande City, Texas; and the gently rolling hills of Starr County are part of his heritage. In 1905, Roel's grandfather registered the "05" brand, still used today on his 900-acre cattle ranch. Although mainly a cow-calf operation, the focus is moving more toward wildlife. Roel has learned that photographers will pay for access to his wildlife, and he is at the forefront of a fledgling industry.

Photography has been Roel's hobby since his teens, and he remembers developing black and white photos in his makeshift darkroom. He loved to travel to photograph, but seldom saw anything worthwhile at home. Then, a few years ago, he attended a workshop in Florida with famed bird photographer Arthur Morris.

That experience sent him back to Texas to buy better equipment and, for the first time, to discover the birds on the ranch. A small blind on a primitive water hole, a sunflower seed feeder and a new 500mm lens produced some great shots. "I had no idea I had that many birds on the ranch," he joked. "I mailed a collection to Artie and invited him to come visit." Arthur Morris jumped at the chance for viewing Texas birds up close, and has since helped Roel set up photo areas that attract guests from around the world.

Larry Ditto has been selling photos for over 30 years. Through 29 years with the U.S. Fish & Wildlife Service, he lived in several wild beautiful places, and taking photos was logical. The last 10 years were spent in South Texas, where he entered all the VLF contests and always placed near the top. In 2000, with partner, Greg Lasley, he won First Grand Prize.

This contest he worked alone, spending about 80 days in the field. Why so much time and effort? "Competition," Larry answers, smiling. "It's a chance to beat the best. And, the contest forces you to stay focused and shoot more, so you accumulate more stock." He says co-winning the 2000 contest has greatly helped his status as a professional photographer.

Now retired, the Texas A&M-trained biologist observes, "You don't know how little you know until you take up photography. To become a good nature photographer, you first have to become a good naturalist."

He especially enjoys visiting a ranch and, through photography, helping the landowner see and understand the life cycles that exist on the land. He's seen the contest open doors of understanding and move a whole family into fresh enthusiasm for the treasures of their land.

As for his experience on the Ramírez Ranch, he says, "No one could have asked for a more cooperative landowner."

–Audrey G. Martin

The male, with his dark black body and bright red wing patches, is much showier than the drab brown female. These black birds form huge flocks in the winter, flying by the thousands in a solid dark mass. They adapt as well to suburban areas as to the countryside.

Canon EOS 3 with 500mm lens and 1.4x teleconverter; 1/250 sec at f5.6; Fuji Velvia 50

Red-winged Blackbird

FIRST PLACE, Blackbirds, Jays, Orioles, Tanagers

Paper Wasp

SECOND PLACE, Ants, Bees, Wasps & Other Social Insects

Paper Wasps are strikingly patterned. They perform necessary functions in the wild by pollinating many species of flowers.

Canon EOS 3 with 300mm lens; 1/250 sec at f14; Kodak E100VS

Pyrrhuloxia

THIRD PLACE, Buntings, Cardinals, Grosbeaks, Pyrrhuloxias

The female Pyrrhuloxia's yellow bill is one of the characteristics that distinguishes it from the closely related Northern Cardinal. It frequents country fence rows and clumps of brush.

Canon EOS 3 with 500mm lens and 2x teleconverter; 1/500 sec at f11; Fuji Velvia 100

The Greater Roadrunner is in reality a rather fast bird. It often hunts lizards, small birds and other such animals by surprising them from a perching spot. These birds have even been known to leap straight up to catch hummingbirds.

Canon EOS 3 with 500mm lens and 1.4x teleconverter; 1/250 sec at f5.6; Fuji Velvia 50

Greater Roadrunner
FIRST PLACE, Anis, Cuckoos, Roadrunners
SECOND PLACE, Birds Division

Crested Caracara

FIRST PLACE, Birds of Prey I

Majestic in their own right, the Crested Caracara rules
the South Texas brush country. These beautiful birds
are closely related to the falcon family.

Canon EOS 3 with 500mm lens and 1.4x teleconverter; 1/250 sec at f8; Fuji Velvia 50

Raccoon

SECOND PLACE, Mustelids & Raccoons

The Raccoon, with his trademark tail ringed in white and black, is at home in trees and on the ground. It may use an old log as a den but does not mind a ground burrow for a home.

Canon EOS 3 with 500mm lens; 1/250 at f8; Kodak E100VS

Golden-fronted Woodpecker

SECOND PLACE, All Other Birds

The handsome male can be distinguished from his mate by the red patch on top of his crown. Attaching orange halves to tree branches will attract this bird to your backyard.

Canon EOS 3 with 500mm lens and 2x teleconverter; 1/80 sec at f8; Fuji Velvia 50

Gulf Coast Toad

SECOND PLACE, Sunrise/Sunset

Day's end brings out a new group of animals, including the Gulf Coast Toad, ready to spend the night in search of sustenance. These toads frequently emerge in the daytime after it rains.

Canon EOS 3 with 300mm lens and 1.4x teleconverter; 1/60 sec at f16; Fuji Velvia 50

White-tailed Deer

SECOND PLACE, White-tailed Deer

Young bucks and does alike take advantage of small ponds scattered throughout the South Texas brush country. The White-tailed Deer is the largest native mammal in the area.

Canon EOS 3 with 300mm lens; 1/60 sec at f5.6; Fuji Velvia 50

Nature is the one place where miracles not only happen,
but happen every day.

–Thomas Wolfe

Fifth Grand Prize

Photographer: **Tom Urban**

Landowner: **King Ranch, Inc.**
Encino Division

Sprawling across 825,000 acres of deep South Texas, the vast King Ranch is a vital reservoir for native creatures and migratory birds. The ranch has been an outstanding steward of the land, successfully integrating wildlife management and cattle production. Migrating songbirds, raptors and waterfowl, already diminishing due to habitat loss, would suffer an even steeper decline without the oak mottes, prairies and wetlands the ranch provides for resting and feeding during migration.

The life of a Valley Land Fund Contest consistent winner is deeply attuned to the King Ranch and its dedication to wildlife. Tom Urban, the 2004 Fifth Grand Prize winner, manages the Venada Camp on the Encino Division of the Ranch. His association with the Ranch began when, while he was still in college, he participated in several studies there. After a brief tenure with the National Park Service, which sparked his interest in outdoor photography, Tom became the first lease manager on the 20,000-acre Venada Camp when the King Ranch opened the property to hunting in the fall of 1979.

Recently, Tom's prize-winning photography, his beloved King Ranch, and the attention to South Texas wildlife all came together in a remarkable way.

During the King Ranch's 150th birthday celebration in 2003, Caroline "Cina" Forgason, great-great granddaughter of Captain Richard King, and co-editor Dr. Paul Genho, King Ranch vice president for ranching operations, worked with Urban to publish

Wildlife on the King Ranch, a commemorative pictorial exclusively featuring 300 of Urban's wildlife photos.

Ms. Forgason commented on the emergence of the volume. "Our whole family appreciates what The Valley Land Fund has accomplished over the years, and their books actually inspired us to publish *Wildlife on the King Ranch*."

Of his connections with all the entities, Urban observed, "I am very grateful to the ranch for allowing me to participate in The Valley Land Fund Contest. I have been working on the ranch for 25 years, and I am still in awe of the wildlife here."

In addition to the many year-round duties of a hunting camp manager, Tom has spent countless hours documenting the tremendous biodiversity of the ranch. "I enjoy the remoteness and serenity of the camp. I also appreciate the amazing wildlife diversity."

The remarkable photographs of Tom Urban reveal not only the astounding diversity of wildlife on the King Ranch, but they also celebrate one man's life work on the land he loves.

"I'm grateful for the opportunity to share my photographs, and it would not have been possible without the outstanding land stewardship of the King Ranch."

–Richard Moore

The Western Coachwhip is a fast-moving diurnal species that is frequently seen foraging near brush lands. Adult coloration can vary, including gray, brown and yellow and even with a reddish phase. They climb readily and can be found searching for prey among the thorny branches of trees and shrubs.

Western Coachwhip
FIRST PLACE, Non-venomous Snakes II

Canon F1 with 400mm lens; 1/250 sec at f4; Kodak E100VS

Texas Tortoise

FIRST PLACE, Tortoises & Turtles

One of the favorite foods of the Texas Tortoise is the Prickly Pear Cactus fruit, locally called "tunas." When not in fruit, the pads or "nopalitos" are also eaten. The tortoise shell can be scarred and blackened when grass or brush fires sweep through their habitat.

Canon F1 with 400mm f2.8 lens; 1/250 sec at f4; Fuji Velvia 50

Rio Grande Leopard Frog

THIRD PLACE, Frogs & Toads

Rio Grande Leopard Frogs will use anything available as a perching site near water. When they see a potential predator approach, they leap into the deeper water while making a yelping vocalization.

Canon F1 with 400mm f2.8 lens; 1/60 sec at f8; Kodak E100VS

White-tailed Deer

THIRD PLACE, White-tailed Deer

Notifying competing males and possible mates of his presence, the buck carries magnificent antlers to back up his call. This majestic animal is a sight not to be forgotten.

Canon F1 with 400mm f2.8 lens; 1/125 sec at f2.8; Kodak E100VS

Crested Caracara

THIRD PLACE, Birds of Prey I

The bird on the Mexican flag might be the Crested Caracara; it might be the Golden Eagle. Historians aren't sure. In any case both Caracaras and Golden Eagles will eat snakes, just like the bird on the flag.

Canon F1 with 400mm f2.8 lens; 1/125 sec at f2.8; Kodak E100VS

Nature will bear the closest inspection. She invites us to lay our eye level with her smallest leaf and take an insect view of its plain.

–*Henry David Thoreau*

In the end, our society will be defined not only by what we created,
but by what we refused to destroy.

–*John Sawhill*

South Texas Shootout
PORTFOLIOS
additional PRIZE WINNERS

Scissor-tailed Flycatcher

THIRD PLACE, Flycatchers & Kingbirds

Feeding young takes much of the parent's time until the young Scissor-tailed Flycatcher strikes out on its own. This beautiful bird is well known for its long flowing tail and acrobatic flight.

Photographer: Sonny Manley
Landowner: Starr Feedyards

Canon EOS with 500mm lens and 2x teleconverter; Fuji Velvia 50

Vermilion Flycatcher

SECOND PLACE, Flycatchers & Kingbirds

The male sports the brightest of red, contrasted by areas of jet black, making it one of the showiest birds. Vermilion Flycatchers can be found in open places such as meadows and pastures.

Canon EOS 3 with 500mm lens and 2x teleconverter; Fuji Velvia 50

Black-tailed Jackrabbit

FIRST PLACE, Rabbits & Hares

This agile inhabitant of the arid brush country serves as a food animal for many predators. It relies on its ability to blend with the surroundings to escape detection. Once spotted, however, a jackrabbit can flee at speeds of up to 35 miles an hour, covering 20 feet in a single hop. The large ears help it keep cool in the heat.

Canon EOS 3 with 500mm lens and 1.4x teleconverter; Fuji Provia 100

Curve-billed Thrasher

SECOND PLACE, Catbirds, Mockingbirds, Shrikes, Thrashers, Thrushes

The Curve-billed Thrasher lives in the arid brush country and is a mimic with a large repertoire of sounds and calls. A grasshopper is surely a tasty meal for the foraging thrasher, whose diet is primarily smaller insects and berries.

Canon EOS 3 with 500mm IS lens and 2x teleconverter; Fuji Provia 100

Lark Sparrow

THIRD PLACE, Sparrows & Towhees

Perched on fence wire, telephone lines and open tree branches, this bird shows its beautiful head pattern with rich colors and sings a melodious song. The Lark Sparrow, like most South Texas sparrows, resides in open grassy habitats.

Canon EOS 3 with 500mm lens and 2x teleconverter; 1/100 sec at f10; Fuji Velvia 50

A cunning opportunist, the Coyote will feast on just about any animal or plant material it can find. Although much maligned as a livestock killer, the Coyote would rather hunt rabbits and other small mammals. Adults are monogamous and jointly raise their young. Its well-known howl evokes a sense of wild.

Canon EOS 3 with 500mm lens; f4; Fuji Velvia 100

Coyote
FIRST PLACE, Coyotes & Foxes

Scaled Quail

FIRST PLACE, Chachalacas, Quail, Turkeys

Mostly a western bird species in South Texas, the Scaled Quail is becoming less abundant. The "cotton top," as it is often called, is a bird of more scrubby ranch landscape and is a challenge to hunters, as it runs rapidly along the ground instead of flushing in flight.

Canon EOS 3 with 500mm f4 IS lens and 2x teleconverter; Fuji Velvia 50

Greater Roadrunner

SECOND PLACE, Anis, Cuckoos, Roadrunners

The *Paisano*, as it is known in Spanish, can run along easily at 15 miles per hour and speed up considerably to catch a fast lizard. It eats a remarkable array of prey, including snakes, small birds, grasshoppers, beetles and snails.

Canon EOS 3 with 500mm lens and 2x teleconverter; Fuji Sensia 100

Cactus Wren

SECOND PLACE, Gnatcatchers, Kinglets, Nuthatches, Titmice, Verdins, Vireos, Warblers, Wrens

The Cactus Wren is the largest in the wren family and aptly named, as it resides in dense cactus patches. As with other wrens, its raucous scolding call can easily be heard long before one enters its territory.

Canon EOS 3 with 500mm lens and 2x teleconverter; Fuji Velvia 50

Blackbuck

SECOND PLACE, All Other Mammals

An introduced antelope species to South Texas ranch country, this exotic mammal was brought mainly as a game animal. The beautiful color pattern of the male is highlighted by his white "eye rings."

Photographer: Michael Delesantro
Landowner: Daniel L. and Tricia Drefke, Skipper Ranch

Canon EOS 1V with 600mm f4 IS lens; Fuji Provia 100

Western Diamondback Rattlesnake

THIRD PLACE, Venomous Snakes

Western Diamondback Rattlesnakes have large fangs enclosed in a sheath. Their size enables them to deliver a large volume of venom in a single bite. Females can give birth to 25 live young in a litter, usually born in late summer.

Canon EOS 1V with 180mm f3.5L macro lens; Fuji Provia 100

Moth Caterpillar

FIRST PLACE, Camouflage

Nature's creations are superbly adapted to their environments. The inchworm, a moth caterpillar, blends in perfectly with the plant stalk on which it climbs.

Canon EOS 1V with 180mm and f3.5L macro lens; Fuji Provia 100

Bobcat

SECOND PLACE, Wild Cats

Nighttime brings out a new group of animals to replace the day-dwelling species. A water hole at dusk may offer a glimpse of a thirsty Bobcat. Bobcats have a litter of from two to seven kittens, usually born in April. The mother teaches them to hunt and survive until fall when the young leave to seek their own territories.

Photographers: Randall Ennis & Beto Gutierrez
Landowner: San Pedro Ranch

Nikon F5 with 500mm lens; 1/250 sec at f4; Velvia 100

Pyrrhuloxia

SECOND PLACE, Buntings, Cardinals, Grosbeaks, Pyrrhuloxias

"Old Fiery Crooked-bill" (a translation of its name), the Pyrrhuloxia is a closely related cousin of the Cardinal, but sports a yellow rather than an orange bill. The male's plumage only shows splotches of red on its otherwise gray body.

Canon EOS 1V with 500mm f4 IS lens and 1.4x teleconverter; 1/125 sec at f11; Kodak E100VS

Funnel Web Spider

SECOND PLACE, Spiders

Obviously named for its unique web, this spider creates a wonderful home by spinning a round tube low on the ground.

Nikon F5 with 200mm macro lens; 1/250 sec at f16; Velvia 100

Eastern Cottontail

SECOND PLACE, Rabbits & Hares

The Eastern Cottontail is the most numerous and widespread rabbit and is well known for its white tail resembling a cotton ball. It thrives wherever green vegetation provides food or cover. One cottontail of twenty lives out its first year. Populations are maintained through amazing reproduction.

Canon EOS 1V with 500mm f4 IS lens and 1.4x teleconverter; 1/125 sec at f8; Kodak E100VS

Crested Caracara

FIRST PLACE, Sunrise/Sunset
THIRD PLACE, Special Categories Division

As the sun sets over the South Texas brush country, the inhabitants search out their favorite roosting spots. The Crested Caracara, stately as it is, appears even more regal in this setting.

Photographer: Kermit Denver Laird
Landowner: Darrell and Suzie Thompson, Speer Ranch

Nikon F5 with 600mm f4 AFS lens; Kodak E100VS

Bullock's Oriole

THIRD PLACE, Blackbirds, Jays, Orioles, Tanagers

Orioles are the brightest colored of the blackbird family. Loved for their vivid orange and yellow colors, they can add cheer to any day, and just might visit a backyard if orange slices are offered as a treat.

Nikon F5 with 600mm f4 AFS lens and extension tube; Kodak E100VS

Land Snail

SECOND PLACE, All Other Arthropods & Snails

Snails move like worms, by stretching and contracting their bodies. They produce mucus which reduces friction and the risk of injury as they slide along prickly surfaces.

Nikon F5 with 200mm f4 lens; 1/250 sec at f16; Kodak E100VS

Strawberry Cactus

THIRD PLACE, Landscape/Waterscape

The colors of late spring in the South Texas brush country are complemented by the many native cactus species. The Strawberry Cactus, locally referred to as "Pitaya," is a breathtaking sight in an otherwise sparse setting.

Photographer: **Kermit Denver Laird**
Landowner: **Speer Ranch**

Nikon F5 with 24-120mm lens; f16; Kodak E100VS

Common Pauraque

SECOND PLACE, Hummingbirds, Nightjars, Swallows, Swifts

Nightjars feed on flying insects at dusk and dawn. A South Texas specialty found nowhere else in the United States, the pauraque roosts mostly on the ground, hiding in leaf litter. Fledglings learn to fly within a short time in order to escape from predators.

Photographer: **Bill Burns**
Landowner: **Bill Burns Ranch**

Canon EOS 3 with 100-400mm lens; 1/250 sec at f8; Fuji Velvia 100

Also known as the Crayfish, or Crawdad, this feisty little arthropod can be found in many large bodies of fresh water.

Canon EOS 3 with 100-400mm lens; 1/375 sec at f7; Fuji Velvia 100

Crawfish

FIRST PLACE, All Other Arthropods & Snails

Anhinga

SECOND PLACE, Water Birds II

Nicknamed the "snake bird," the Anhinga swims with only the slender neck, head and bill above water, appearing more like a snake than a bird. Unlike other water birds, the Anhinga's feathers absorb water, forcing it to dry and preen them in the sun.

Canon EOS 3 with 500mm lens; 1/400 sec at f6; Fuji Velvia 100

Double-crested Cormorant

THIRD PLACE, Water Birds II

A superb fisherman, the Double-crested Cormorant can be found diving for prey in any waterway, from ditches to ocean.

Canon EOS 3 with 500mm lens; 1/350 sec at f8; Fuji Velvia 100

Northern Bobwhite

THIRD PLACE, Chachalacas, Quail, Turkeys

The male Northern Bobwhite sports a white face and throat while the female bears a tan coloring. The Bobwhite is a coveted game species and inhabits grassy fields, where it feeds on berries and seeds of many native plants. Its call sounds like "bob white."

Canon EOS 3 with 500mm lens; 1/350 sec at f8; Fuji Velvia 100

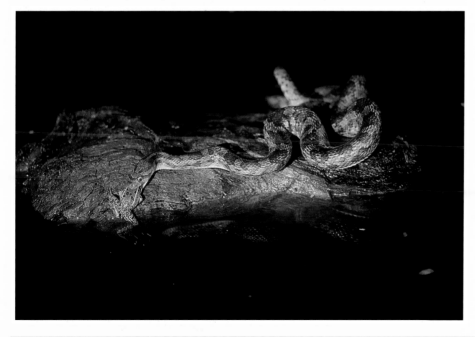

Great Plains Rat Snake

SECOND PLACE, Non-venomous Snakes II

Great Plains Rat Snakes are common in South Texas. Active by day or night, they feed largely on rodents and birds and occasionally on frogs. Rat Snakes are valuable in controlling rodent populations around barns and homes.

Canon EOS 3 with 100-400mm lens; Fuji Velvia 100

Killdeer

FIRST PLACE, Action

The beauty of wildlife in the South Texas brush land is often displayed at the many watering holes scattered about the countryside. The Killdeer can be found in drier areas but will take an opportunity for a refreshing bath.

Photographer: John Pickles
Landowners: Sharon R. Waite, Metz & Waite Farm and William R. Buchholz

The Black-necked Stilt, one of the most glamorous shorebirds with its contrasting colors and bright red legs, makes a simple nest by hollowing out a small cup near the shore. It's easy to see where this long-legged bird derives its name.

Canon EOS 1V with 600mm lens and 1.4x teleconverter; 1/60 sec at f5.6; Fuji Provia

Black-necked Stilt
FIRST PLACE, Shorebirds

Nine-banded Armadillo

FIRST PLACE, Animal Babies

The Nine-banded Armadillo is normally out and about during night hours. A sleepy youngster might venture out from time to time to check its surroundings.

Canon EOS 1V with 28-135mm lens; 1/125 sec at f5.6; Fuji Provia

Great Plains Rat Snake

THIRD PLACE, Non-venomous Snakes II

The Great Plains Rat Snake may try to bluff predators by pretending to be a rattlesnake. When cornered it may vibrate its tail like a rattlesnake and strike with impressive speed. However, its bite is not venomous and it must constrict its prey.

Canon EOS 1V with 28-135mm lens and; 1/60 sec at f8; Fuji Provia

Merriam's Pocket Mouse

THIRD PLACE, Rodents

The nocturnal Merriam's Pocket Mouse inhabits arid as well as brushy areas, where it burrows a den near a cactus or shrub. It is able to extract its water needs from the seeds that it eats.

Canon EOS 1V with 35-135mm lens; 1/60 sec at f8; Fuji Provia

Golden-fronted Woodpecker

FIRST PLACE, All Other Birds

One of the many birds that enjoy the fruit of the Prickly Pear Cactus, this bird is a frequent visitor to the "tunas." The most common of woodpeckers in South Texas, the Golden-fronted feels at home in city yards or out in the countryside.

Photographers: Mary Jo Bogatto Janovsky and Mary Donahue
Landowner: RGV Outdoors Center

Western Diamondback Rattlesnake

FIRST PLACE, Venomous Snakes

Equipped with a heat-sensitive sensory organ on each side of the head, rattlesnakes can locate warm-blooded prey and strike even in the dark. If you hear a rattlesnake shaking its rattle, back away. The snake is issuing a warning.

Black-necked Stilt

THIRD PLACE, Shorebirds

A true show-stopper, the Black-necked Stilt sports a natural tuxedo.
He probes the bottoms of shallow ponds
and shorelines for tiny morsels.

Photographers: Mary Jo Bogatto Janovsky and Mary Donahue
Landowner: RGV Outdoors Center

American Lady

THIRD PLACE, Butterflies II

Butterfly patterns can be simple or intricate in design, such as on this
American Lady. Even though brightly and colorfully patterned,
this butterfly can blend with its surroundings, thanks to
the cryptic designs on its underwings.

Photographer: Dennis Erhart
Landowners: Ken and Barbara Weaver and
                          Kent and G'Anne Weaver, Weaver Ranch

Canon EOS 1N with 180mm macro lens; 1/60 sec at f16; Fuji Provia

Texas Spiny Lizard

FIRST PLACE, Anoles, Geckos, Lizards & Skinks

Texas Spiny Lizards are usually seen climbing on tree trunks, logs or walls of buildings. The female is recognized by her light-colored chin and abdomen, while the male has a bright blue underside.

Canon EOS 1N with 180mm macro lens; 1/125 sec at f16; Fuji Provia

Tiger Salamander

FIRST PLACE, Salamanders & Sirens
THIRD PLACE, Reptiles & Amphibians Division

Tiger Salamanders can be found in the sandy soils of the northern Rio Grande Valley. They are usually seen in their larval aquatic form in potholes and ponds not stocked with fish. Their external gills disappear when they mature into their adult terrestrial form.

Canon EOS 1N with 180mm macro lens; 1/60 sec at f11; Fuji Velvia

Queen

SECOND PLACE, Butterflies II

One of the most common butterflies in South Texas, the Queen can be seen nectaring at bright flowers both in the wild and in the city. The Queen caterpillar feeds on milkweed and milkweed vine.

Canon EOS 1N with 180mm macro lens; 1/125 sec at f11; Fuji Provia

Cattle Egret

THIRD PLACE, Wading Birds

The Cattle Egret is an opportunist, following feeding livestock or plows to seize available insects. The orangish hue to its head indicates breeding plumage.

Canon EOS 1N with 600mm lens; 1/125 sec at f5.6; Fuji Provia 100

Roseate Spoonbill

FIRST PLACE, Wading Birds

The spoonbill, one of the most colorful and fascinating birds in South Texas, can be seen feeding along the coastal shores and in freshwater inland lakes.

Photographer: Rex Hewitt
Landowner: Buena Vista Ranch

Canon 1V with 600mm lens and 1.4x teleconverter; 1/500 sec at f5.6; Fuji Velvia 100

Javelina

THIRD PLACE, Javelinas

The native "wild pig" of the ranch country is rather small, but not to be underestimated, owning a set of formidable tusks which it uses to defend its young, fight off outsiders, and root for tasty morsels.

Photographers: Irene Hinke-Sacilotto and Gary Carlton
Landowner: H. Yturria Ranch

Nikon F100 with 300mm f2.8 lens; 1/250 sec at f2.8; Fuji Provia 100

Red-eared Slider

SECOND PLACE, Tortoises & Turtles

The Red Eared Slider is the most common turtle in South Texas and is named for the red patch behind the eye. Sliders feed on insects, worms, snails, small fish and aquatic plants.

Nikon F5 with 600mm f4 lens; 1/750 sec at f5.6; Fuji Provia 100

Roseate Spoonbill

SECOND PLACE, Wading Birds

Sometimes referred to as the Texas Flamingo, the Spoonbill derives its name from the shape of the bill it moves back and forth in the water to filter out small crustaceans.

Nikon F100 with 500mm f4 lens; 1/300 sec at f4; Fuji Provia 100

Javelina

SECOND PLACE, Javelinas

The Javelina is most active during mornings and evenings when it wanders the brush country in small bands for such native foods as Prickly Pear Cactus and Mesquite beans.

Nikon F100 with 300mm f2.8 lens; 1/250 sec at f2.8; Fujichrome Provia 100

Sunset

THIRD PLACE, Sunrise/Sunset

Reflected in a still country pond, the setting sun is a reminder of another day's passing for the animals calling the ranch lands of South Texas home. The quiet peace is a perfect close to a day spent in such surroundings.

Photographers: Irene Hinke-Sacilotto and Gary Carlton
Landowner: H. Yturria Ranch

Nikon F100 with 20-35mm lens; 1/200 sec at f2.8; Fujichrome Provia 100

Garden Spider

THIRD PLACE, Patterns

The heavy dew of a South Texas spring morning creates the most wonderful patterns. The web of the Garden Spider is often found glistening in the early morning light.

Photographer: Bill M. Campbell, MD
Landowner: The Cozad Ranch

Nikon F5 with 200mm micro f4 lens; 1/15 sec at f16; Fuji Velvia

Mediterranean Gecko

FIRST PLACE, All Other Reptiles

The Mediterranean Gecko was introduced from northern Africa and has been a reported resident of South Texas since the late 1950s. Populations have now spread northward to Kansas and Missouri.

Nikon F5 with 200mm micro lens; Fuji Velvia

Yucca

SECOND PLACE, Landscape/Waterscape

A brush country sunset brings a day to its close and refreshes the soul for another day. Yuccas dotting the countryside are sometimes referred to as Spanish Daggers due to their sharply pointed leaves.

Photographer: Bill Caskey and Omar García
Landowner: Varal Ranches, Ltd.

Nikon F5 with 17-35mm f2.8 lens; Fuji Provia 100

Reticulated Collared Lizard

THIRD PLACE, Anoles, Geckos, Lizards, Skinks

Reticulated Collared Lizards are found only in the drier parts of South Texas and Northeastern Mexico. They can be seen basking on top of rocks or mud clods early in the day. After warming up, they minimize their heat absorption by raising their toes and opening their mouths.

Nikon F5 with 500mm f4 lens; Fuji Provia 100

Spotted Ground Squirrel

FIRST PLACE, Rodents
THIRD PLACE, Mammals Division
PEOPLE'S CHOICE

Although officially a rodent, with its comical antics who couldn't love the Spotted Ground Squirrel? Racing across the ground only to stop and look around, this little fellow feels just as well at home under rock and root.

Photographers: David Cantú & Arnoldo Cantú
Landowner: A. Cantú Farms

Nikon F100 with 14mm rectilinear lens; 1/250 sec at f16; Fuji Provia 100

This flashy spider is a common resident in colorful gardens or patches of wildflowers. It performs an important task by feeding on visiting insects.

Photographer: Gary McHale
Landowner: H. Yturria Ranch

Nikon F80 with 200mm f4 lens; 1/180 sec at f22; Kodak E100VS

Green Lynx Spider
FIRST PLACE, Spiders

Blister Beetle

SECOND PLACE, Beetles

The family group of beetles referred to as Blister Beetles is very colorful. The adults most often feed on flower petals, while larvae are predatory.

Nikon F80 with 200mm f4 lens; 1/180 sec at f16; Kodak E100VS

Red Velvet Mite

SECOND PLACE, All Other Arachnids

The Red Velvet Mite is aptly named for its velvety appearance and can really stand out from its leaf-littered habitat. Tiny in size, it has quite a reputation among South Texas insects, sometimes attacking prey much larger than itself.

Nikon F80 with 200mm f4 lens; 1/180 sec at f32; Kodak E100VS

Spotted Sandpiper
SECOND PLACE, Shorebirds

Bobbing its way along inland shorelines, the Sandpiper sports an easily recognizable plumage during its breeding season. Mostly a winter resident in South Texas, it loses its spots during those months, but the constant bobbing of its tail helps identify this species.

Photographer: Ken Allaman
Landowner: Rio Grande Container Game Ranch

Nikon F5 with 500mm lens at f5.6; Fuji Velvia 100

Argiope
SECOND PLACE, Patterns

Females rest with their heads pointed toward the ground. Few females survive to maturity, but those that do often eat their male mate, even though he checks with her by twitching her web to see if it's safe to approach.

Photographers: Larry L. and Nancy C. Von Behren
Landowner: Douglas Hardie

Nikon F5 with 200mm micro lens; 1/60 sec at f8; E100VS

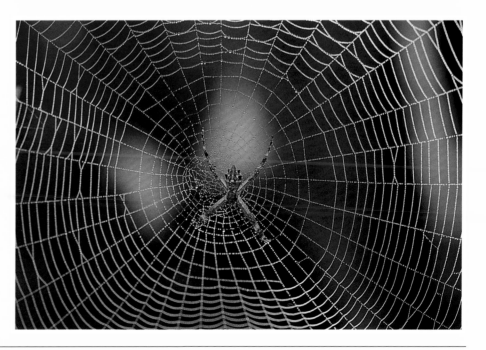

Javelina

FIRST PLACE, Javelinas

Named for its whitish "Collar," the Collared Peccary is better known as the Javelina in South Texas. The range of this pig-like mammal is limited to the southern areas of Texas, Arizona and New Mexico.

Photographer: Barbara Baird
Landowner: John and Audrey Martin

Canon EOS 3 with 500mm f4 lens and 1.4x teleconverter; 1/3 sec at f11; Kodak E100VS

Mexican Ground Squirrel

SECOND PLACE, Rodents

A master at burrowing, the Mexican Ground Squirrel sports a beautiful color pattern with nine rows of white squarish spots. This little fellow forages on seeds, roots, insects and stems.

Canon EOS 3 with 300mm f2.8 lens and 2x teleconverter; f5.6; Kodak E100VS

Coyote

SECOND PLACE, Coyotes & Foxes

The Coyote, related to wolves and domestic dogs, is more regal than portrayed in cartoons. It is a fast sleek hunter that has learned to adapt to all situations it encounters. It deserves our respect.

Canon EOS 3 with 500mm f4 lens and 1.4x teleconverter; f8; Kodak E100VS

Bobcat

FIRST PLACE, Wild Cats
FIRST PLACE, Mammals Division

A creature of the night, the Bobcat specializes in hunting for small animals such as rabbits and birds. Its ability to stalk almost unnoticed makes it a successful hunter. One is lucky to ever see this cat on the prowl.

Canon EOS 3 with 300mm f2.8 lens and 2x teleconverter; Kodak E100VS

Lincoln's Sparrow

FIRST PLACE, Sparrows & Towhees

The Lincoln's Sparrow hardly wears a top hat, but his distinct facial pattern gives him away even when wet from a bath. This little fellow frequents grass-covered fence lines in brushy areas and, as with most sparrows, is a master at not being seen.

Canon EOS 3 with 300mm f2.8 lens and 2x teleconverter; f5.6; Kodak E100VS

Blue Water Lily

FIRST PLACE, Landscapes/Waterscapes
SECOND PLACE, Special Categories Division

The scenic attractions of South Texas can include a countryside pond created by recent rainfall. The Blue Water Lily, found during wet years throughout the ranch country, adds beauty to any setting.

Photographer: Catherine Evans
Landowner: Payne Ranch

Canon EOS 3 with 100-400 IS lens; Fuji Provia 100

Tiger Salamander
SECOND PLACE, Salamanders & Sirens

No two adult Tiger Salamanders have the same black and yellow color pattern. Adults burrow through sandy soils but can be seen wandering above ground at night during a rain.

Photographer: Joseph Holman
Landowner: Miguel A. and Analicia Q. García, El Devisadero Ranch

Bobcat
THIRD PLACE, Wild Cats

An encounter with a wild Bobcat is a rare unforgettable experience. A rather secretive cat with many different types of habitats, it can surprise you at times in unexpected places.

Red Velvet Mite

THIRD PLACE, All Other Arachnids

These arachnids in adult form feed on soil-dwelling insects like mosquito larvae, springtails and pillbugs. The larval, more pesky form is the nearly invisible critter with the nickname of "chigger."

Photographer: Ted Bragg
Landowners: Santa Cecilia Ranch and Rancho Margo La Coma

Nutria

THIRD PLACE, All Other Mammals

Originally from South America, this aquatic rodent has established itself in the South Texas wild. Feeding on aquatic plants, the Nutria is now considered a pest since it competes with native animals.

Photographers: Paul Denman and Vern Denman
Landowner: Winifred R. Wetegrove, Las Majadas Ranch

Canon 1V with 500mm f4 lens; 1/125 sec at f5.6; Fuji Velvia 100

Coyote

THIRD PLACE, Coyotes & Foxes

The Coyote has been persecuted throughout the country yet does not show signs of disappearing soon. It has learned to adapt to human encroachment better than most wild creatures. Although mostly nocturnal and rather shy, it might be seen at any time of day.

Photographers: Lowell Hudsonpillar and Ken York
Landowners: Larry and Betty Lou Sheerin, La Brisa Ranch

Canon EOS Rebel; Fuji Velvia 50

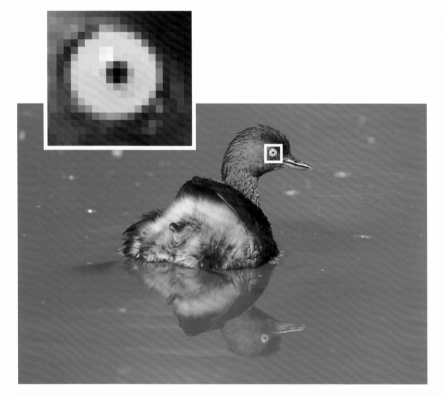

South Texas Shootout
Digital Competition

In recognition of the evolution of digital photography and its importance and legitimacy in the art of wildlife photography, The Valley Land Fund created the 2004 Digital Competition on a trial basis to determine both the potential for high quality images as well as a protocol for the format, submission and judging of these electronic images. Photographers and landowners who were entered in the South Texas Shootout were eligible to enter the Digital Competition and allowed to submit up to 25 images, five in each of five divisions. The images were judged and points were awarded similar to the South Texas Shootout system. Prize money was distributed to the top five winners.

–Bob Simpson

South Texas Shootout
PORTFOLIOS
Digital Competition

First Prize

Photographer: John Pickles

Landowner: Sharon R. Waite, Metz and Waite Farm and William R. Buchholz

Least Bittern

FIRST PLACE, Birds
BEST OF CONTEST

This secretive bird is found primarily along bodies of water with thick stands of reeds and cattails. While standing perfectly still, it raises its neck and head to imitate a cattail stalk as it waits to ambush its fishy prey.

Canon EOS 1D Mark II with 600mm f4 lens and 2x teleconverter; 1/125 sec at f8

Green Kingfisher

THIRD PLACE, Birds

The smallest of the North American kingfishers, the Green Kingfisher patrols the rivers, canals and ponds no further north than South Texas. Though usually heard before seen, this expert fisherman's call sounds like the rapid beating together of stones.

Canon EOS 10D with 100-400mm lens; 1/125 sec at f8

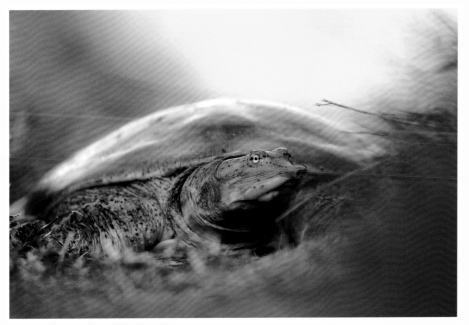

Texas Spiny Softshell

THIRD PLACE, Reptiles & Amphibians

The Texas Spiny Softshell is often found buried in mud or very shallow water with only its eyes and nostrils appearing above the water line. Its shell, devoid of any scales, is leathery and soft enough to bend at the sides and rear.

Canon EOS 1D Mark II with 600mm f4 lens and 2x teleconverter; 1/125 sec at f8

Grasshopper

FIRST PLACE, Insects & Arachnids

Being quite colorful and sporting unique patterns when viewed up close, grasshoppers are an intricate part of the large animal food chain. Many birds, reptiles and small mammals feed on the varied species of grasshoppers found in the wild and in our gardens.

Canon EOS 1D Mark II with 200mm macro lens; 1/60 sec at f5.6

Spotted Ground Squirrel

SECOND PLACE, Mammals

Surveying its surroundings, this fellow is on constant watch for any predatory threats. The Spotted Ground Squirrel is an inhabitant of the semi-open and dry brush country of southern Texas and ranges into other Southwestern states.

Canon EOS 1D Mark II with 600mm f4 lens and 2x teleconveter; 1/125 sec at f8

Second Prize

Photographer: **Bill M. Campbell, MD**
Landowner: **The Cozad Ranch**

Audubon's Oriole

HONORABLE MENTION, Birds

Belonging to one of the most colorful bird families, the Audubon's Oriole is mostly found upriver along the Rio Grande and in the drier western habitats.

Nikon D2H

Rambur's Forktail

HONORABLE MENTION, Insects & Arachnids

Delicate cousins of dragonflies, damselflies live a very similar lifestyle, feeding on mosquitoes and other small creatures. This species is highly variable in its coloration, ranging from blue and green to orange color patterns.

Nikon D2H with 200mm micro lens

Third Prize

Photographer: Gary McHale
Landowner: H. Yturria Ranch

Blister Beetle

SECOND PLACE, Special Categories

In the animal kingdom, beetles make up the largest group or order, with at least 250,000 known kinds. Blister Beetles feed on flowers and leaves of soft plants.

Nikon F80 with 200mm macro f4 lens; 1/180sec at f16; digital

Fourth Prize

Photographer: **Jeremy Woodhouse**
Landowner: **Roberto and Fran Yzaguirre**

Garden Spider

SECOND PLACE, Insects & Arachnids

Weaving their intricate webs creates the perfect food-gathering tool. Garden Spiders can be found around homes and gardens, and are quite useful in catching unwanted pests.

Canon EOS 1Ds with 180mm macro f3.5 lens and 1.4x teleconverter; 1/5 sec at f32; digital

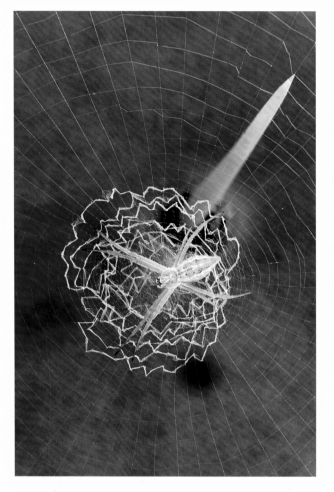

Rio Grande Leopard Frog

SECOND PLACE, Reptiles & Amphibians

Present in almost any habitat with a water source, the Rio Grande Leopard Frog can reproduce in large numbers as soon as water appears, even in normally arid regions. After heavy rainfalls, it may be seen around stock tanks and other small bodies of water.

Canon EOS 1Ds with 600mm f4 lens and 2x teleconverter; 1/30 sec f8; digital

Black-tailed Jackrabbit

FIRST PLACE, Mammals

A wildlife fixture in open brush country, the Black-tailed Jackrabbit is not a rabbit but rather a hare, and is quite the athlete. Despite those big ears its speed and agility may keep it from becoming a Coyote's favorite meal.

Canon EOS 1Ds with 600mm f4 lens and 1.4x teleconverter; 1/320 sec at f5.6; digital

Eastern Cottontail

SECOND PLACE, Special Categories

One of the most common mammals in South Texas, the Eastern Cottontail Rabbit can be found in both the countryside and in urban settings. In town, it will often munch on freshly planted flowers and shrubs.

Canon EOS 1Ds with EF 600mm f4 lens; 1/640 sec at f4; digital

Flame Skimmer

THIRD PLACE, Insects & Arachnids

Dragonflies are generally predatory insects, with chewing mouthparts. Their primary prey is mosquitos and other small insects. Fossil remains with 2.5 feet wingspans have been found.

Canon EOS 1DS with 180mm macro lens and 2x teleconverter; 1/125sec at f8; digital

Fifth Prize

Photographers: **Bill Caskey and Omar García**

Landowner: **Varal Ranches Ltd.**

Not a very common species in South Texas, the American Bullfrog has a large appetite and will eat just about anything that comes its way, including other frogs, snakes and small turtles.

Nikon D1X with 80-400 VR lens; digital

American Bullfrog

FIRST PLACE, Reptiles & Amphibians

White-tailed Kite

SECOND PLACE, Birds

Once known as the Black-shouldered Kite, it was previously named for the black spots in the wings seen when the bird is kiting high above a field searching for small rodent prey.

Photographers: Paul Denman & Vern Denman
Landowner: Winifred R. Wetegrove, Las Majadas Ranch

Canon Digital Rebel with 500mm f4 lens; 1/800 sec at f8; ISO 100

Millipede

THIRD PLACE, Special Categories

Nature's intricate patterns appear in some very unusual animals, such as the Millipede. When threatened, this small arthropod defends itself by rolling into a very tight circle and, if picked up, emits a foul-smelling substance.

Canon Digital Rebel with 180mm macro lens; 1/125 sec at f8

Frog Eggs and Tadpoles
FIRST PLACE, Special Categories

In South Texas springtime, choruses of frogs and toads join with birdsong. Looking carefully in any source of standing water, one can find clusters of frog eggs and developing tadpoles.

Canon Digital Rebel with 180mm macro lens; 1/125 sec at f8; ISO 100

South Texas Shootout Judges

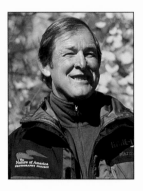

Jeff Foott
Jackson Hole, WY
Jeff Foott Productions

Jeff Foott started out as a marine biologist by training but worked his way into the field of art by photographing landscapes and wildlife. He has created more than 50 films about nature and wildlife, working with the National Geographic Society, Discovery, PBS, the BBC and others. His still photography has been widely published and he has worked on assignment for *National Geographic, Audubon, Sierra Club,* and many nature photo magazines. He served as advisor for *Outdoor Photographer* for many years.

Deborah Free
Pavilion, NY
Photographer/Stock Agency Consultant
Deborah Free - Image Consultant, L.L.C.

Deborah Free, a return judge for the VLF, has been involved in the photography industry for over 17 years. She started and ran Natural Selection Stock Photography agency for over 11 years and has since formed her own consulting company. She has helped set up and restructure a number of stock-related businesses, has been involved in mediations, helped create and implement marketing strategies and is currently co-producing a photography-related book with Jane Kinne. Her knowledge and expertise continue to grow as the industry itself evolves.

Photo by Dan Smith

John Nuhn
Reston, VA
Photo Director
National Wildlife Magazine .

Trained as a journalist, John Nuhn, a self-taught photographer, is the longtime photo editor and now photography director of award-winning *National Wildlife* magazine, the largest circulation nature periodical in the U.S. He oversees all photography for the magazine's three editions. John is a founder and past president of the North America Nature Photography Association and currently president of the NANPA Foundation. He is past chapter president, vice-president and treasurer of the American Society of Picture Professionals. He has been a speaker, panelist and judge at many industry-related forums and events. This is his third time to judge the VLF contest.

Rare Cat Award

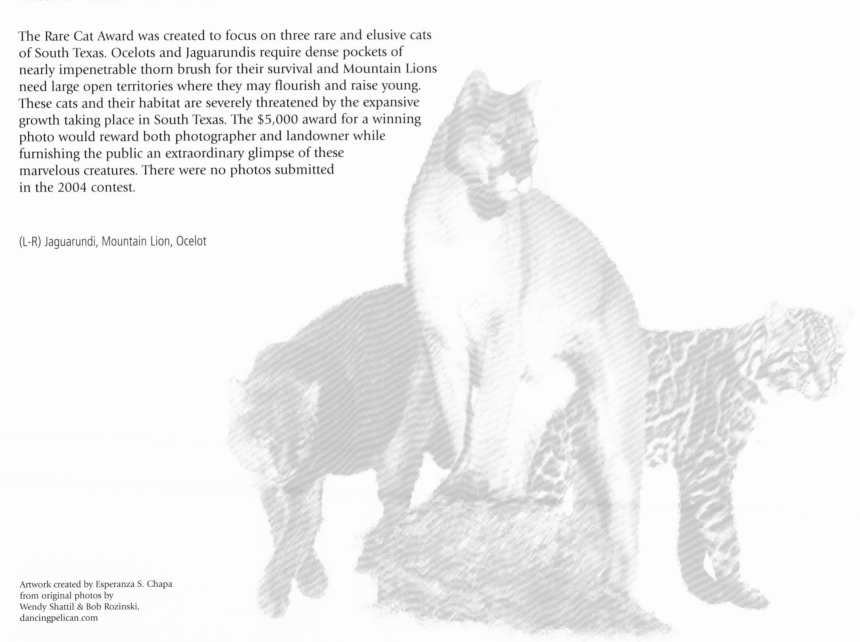

The Rare Cat Award was created to focus on three rare and elusive cats of South Texas. Ocelots and Jaguarundis require dense pockets of nearly impenetrable thorn brush for their survival and Mountain Lions need large open territories where they may flourish and raise young. These cats and their habitat are severely threatened by the expansive growth taking place in South Texas. The $5,000 award for a winning photo would reward both photographer and landowner while furnishing the public an extraordinary glimpse of these marvelous creatures. There were no photos submitted in the 2004 contest.

(L-R) Jaguarundi, Mountain Lion, Ocelot

Artwork created by Esperanza S. Chapa
from original photos by
Wendy Shattil & Bob Rozinski,
dancingpelican.com

Small Tract Competition

Urban and rural back yards and properties of up to 100 acres were the settings for this competition. While probably less rigorous than the Shootout, the goal of this competition was to highlight the importance of small tracts to the conservation of wildlife.

Contestants submitted up to five 35mm slides in each of five divisions: Birds, Mammals, Insects & Arachnids, Reptiles & Amphibians and Special Categories. Three well-known local judges individually scored the submissions, awarding points to each image with bonus points given to those images selected for the top three places in each division. The top five over-all point recipients were designated Grand Prize Winners. Ten landowner/photographer teams shared cash prizes totaling $20,000.

Judges also selected the individual photo that they thought was "Best of Contest" while the "People's Choice" was selected by popular vote at the El Monte awards ceremony.

–Bob Simpson

Small Tract Competition
PORTFOLIOS

First Grand Prize

Photographer: **Suzanne Herzing**

Landowner: **Suzanne Herzing**
Indian Ridge Bed & Breakfast

Suzanne Herzing loves animals. She owns and works in an equestrian center and speaks with excitement and animation when talking about the wildlife she photographed to win the Small Tract First Grand Prize.

Suzanne owns and operates the Indian Ridge Bed and Breakfast in Palmview, an upscale setting where Jimmy and Rosalyn Carter stayed when they came to the Valley on a birding trip in 2004. Originally from Pennsylvania, the past vocations of this multi-talented woman include social worker, singer, and office manager.

Although she started photographing in the 1970s using black and white, Suzanne had never tried her hand at nature photography until just two months before the contest began. Entering as both a landowner and a photographer gave her the opportunity to explore her own property extensively and discover that it was home to many more species than she had previously realized.

Expanding photographic opportunities and improving her skills seemed good reasons for getting involved. She enjoyed her experience but found it difficult time-wise. The riding lessons she gives at her equestrian center are usually given early and late in the day, also prime photography times. Even under these constraints, she will enter again because she feels it is very worthwhile.

In preparation for the contest, she put in a large pond and was amazed by the number of birds that quickly discovered the water. She especially remembers the herons that came in right as she was preparing to leave one day— and had the lens off her camera!

Suzanne has always appreciated the aesthetics of nature, but wildlife photography has kindled a quest for a deeper knowledge about the behavior and interactions of species. She is a Certified Interpretative Guide and is participating in the Texas Master Naturalists program.

Only a mile from US Highway 83, her 20-acre property is now surrounded by subdivisions, and Indian Ridge has become "a little oasis" of native plant and animal life in the midst of explosive development.

And, while it was a thrill to win the competition, she says her main goal was to help motivate people to preserve wildlife habitat. Her goal, and the goal of The Valley Land Fund join right here.

–Mark Gibbs

Black-bellied Whistling-Duck

SECOND PLACE, Special Categories

Once known as the Texas Tree Duck or Texas Whistling Duck because of its habit of nesting in old tree cavities and producing a whistle-like call as it flies, this duck now gets its name from its black-colored belly. The "Black-bellies" are often seen in spring as they search for nest cavities.

Canon EOS 3 with 500mm lens and 1.4 teleconverter at f8; Fuji Provia 100

Swallowtail Caterpillar

SECOND PLACE, Insects & Arachnids

Intricate connections in nature are demonstrated by female butterflies that tend to use very specific host plants on which to lay their eggs. The caterpillars often shed several times as they grow large from feeding on the same host plant.

Canon EOS 3 with 180mm macro lens; Fuji Sensia 100

Red-eared Slider

FIRST PLACE, Reptiles & Amphibians

The Red-eared Slider prefers quiet waters with heavy aquatic vegetation. It is easily identified by the red mark behind its eye. A gentle canoe ride down the Rio Grande will give ample opportunity to spot this turtle basking in the sun along the banks.

Canon EOS 3 with 75-300mm lens and 2x teleconverter; Fuji Sensia 100

We still do not know one thousandth of one percent
of what nature has revealed to us.

–*Albert Einstein*

Second Grand Prize

Photographer: Michael R. Hannisian
Landowner: Suzanne Herzing
              Indian Ridge Bed & Breakfast

Mike Hannisian is a transplanted Texan, having lived most of his life in New Jersey. Mike has been a trial attorney, professor, writer, freelance photographer, and is currently a public school teacher. He has presented programs and been a leader in nature festivals from Maine to Florida and Michigan to Texas. He is a charter member of the RGV Chapter of Master Naturalists and is a Certified Interpretative Guide.

Wildlife photography has been part of his life since 1970 when he took a trip out west where a pair of Ptarmigan piqued his interest. Mike considers himself a serious amateur, although he has sold prints and recently had a showing of his work in Harlingen, Texas. This was his first time to participate in the contest, and he was very pleased with his second place finish.

Picking a location to photograph was not difficult, since he lives at and helps operate the Indian Ridge Bed & Breakfast in Palmview. Suzanne Herzing, the landowner, acquired the 20-acre property in 1993. It now boasts an elegant bed and breakfast and equestrian center, complete with boarding stables and show facilities. Additionally, it attracts lots of wildlife.

In preparation for the contest, Mike and Suzanne built a pond and photo blind. Their labor paid off when a Groove-billed Ani showed up at the pond the day after it was filled. Mike feels he improved his photography skills and enhanced his appreciation for the land through his participation in the contest.

Working with The Valley Land Fund as director when he first came to the Valley gave Mike an understanding of its conservation goals. He believes those goals are enhanced by the contest, as it encourages people to value the land and wildlife of the area. For the next contest, he and Suzanne plan to work toward further revegetation of the property using native plants to attract still more species.

The bed and breakfast has the largest residential swimming pool in the Valley, around which Suzanne has added butterfly gardens. And she is planting a 12-foot-wide perimeter around the property as a corridor for wildlife.

"An enjoyable experience" is how Mike described his participation in the contest, with the most difficult aspect being forced to cut the number of photographic entries down to only 25. In the future, Mike hopes to do more nature writing and photography.

–Mark Gibbs

Couch's Kingbird

THIRD PLACE, Birds

A bird special to deep South Texas, the Couch's Kingbird is almost impossible to tell apart from its cousin, the Tropical Kingbird, unless you hear their call. Often seen perched on fence lines or power lines along country roads, these flycatchers are waiting for a tasty meal to fly by.

Canon EOS 3 with 500mm f4 lens and 1.4X teleconverter; Fuji Sensia 100

Eastern Cottontail

FIRST PLACE, Mammals

It is always a special treat to see a rabbit sitting motionless as you walk past. Eastern Cottontails are fairly easy to locate while nature-watching in almost any habitat in the area. They often rely on their instinct to sit motionless until danger passes.

Canon EOS 3 with 75-300 mm lens; Fuji Sensia 100

Adopt the pace of nature: her secret is patience.

–*Ralph Waldo Emerson*

Third Grand Prize

Photographer: Victor E. Sanchez

Landowner: Amy and Kenneth Johnson
            El Montecito

It was overgrazed pasture just eight years ago, but now "El Montecito" is a nature lover's delight. Located just north of busy SH 107 in McAllen, the 20 secluded acres offer a haven for wildlife in an otherwise suburban landscape. That's what Victor Sanchez saw when he attended a "Meet the Judges" party in 2002 and knew he had to photograph here in 2004.

Victor is a high school band director who won the Second Grand Prize in the 2002 Small Tract Competition and was back in 2004, with more enthusiasm, more equipment, and some new leafy camouflage clothing.

Amy and Kenneth Johnson are committed to continued revegetation of their property. "It's really not that hard to do," Amy says, smiling. "The birds bring the plants and the plants bring the birds." And then they put in the half-acre pond and that became the magnet for wildlife; the coyote that comes at sundown, the raccoons, owls, roadrunners and rabbits – all are at home here.

Amy loves the space, solitude, peace and tranquility of their property, and thinks that there should be more emphasis on the small tracts. "It doesn't matter how small they are, they can still benefit wildlife," she says. "It's all about education." She recalls how her young nephews saw their first tadpoles and frogs at "El Montecito" and how thrilled they were.

The Johnsons have been supporters of The Valley Land Fund for some ten years, and in January 2005 Amy began her term as president of the board. They have hosted the "Meet the Judges" party for three contests and in 2004 turned over their guesthouse for a month to Gabrielle Salazar, a 16-year-old Youth Contest participant from North Carolina.

Kenneth spends his days at Johnson Brothers Construction Co. and tries to counsel developers and engineers to leave more trees and to landscape with native plants. Sometimes he's successful.

For a time, Victor's success in photographing the Eastern Cottontail seemed doubtful. The rabbit would never let Victor too close before dashing into the brush. But on the day that Victor brought his two-year-old son, the child walked right up to the rabbit and they appeared to communicate, as only children and animals can.

"I can walk down a trail without a camera and just enjoy the view and the animals," Victor says. "But when I photograph what I see, it tells a story that I can share with other people."

What else did he learn from the experience? "Leafy camouflage doesn't defend against cactus."

–Audrey G. Martin

Millipede

THIRD PLACE, Special Categories

Intricate shapes and forms abound in nature and looking around one might find millipedes rolling up into their defense position. Surprises are found around every mesquite motte and across every pond, so one must always stay vigilant for the next wonderful sight.

Canon EOS 3 with 180mm f3.5 macro lens; Fuji Velvia 50

Eastern Cottontail

THIRD PLACE, Mammals

Adult Eastern Cottontails feed on most soft tissue plants and love many garden varieties that are freshly planted. One of five cottontails native to the United States, they dig underground and maintain emergency exits to their burrows.

Canon EOS 3 with 600mm f4 lens; 1/200 sec at f5.6; Fuji Velvia 100

Fourth Grand Prize

Photographer: Luciano E. Guerra

Landowner: Luciano E. Guerra

Luciano Guerra is a veteran of Valley Land Fund Wildlife Photo Contests. The 48-year-old Mission resident netted three winning photographs in the 1994 contest, a second place with a spider photograph in 1996, and an honorable mention in the 1998 contest.

"So I was getting progressively worse," he said, a hearty laugh breaking from his throat. "It was very disappointing."

In the 2004 contest, his shot of a Buff-bellied Hummingbird captured the Fourth Grand Prize in the Small Tract Competition.

"It took hundreds of hummingbird photographs to get that one," he said proudly. "A judge told me I was the only one in the Small Tract Competition who received a perfect score."

Luciano planted his nearly half-acre backyard with Bougainvilleas and cactus, Lantana and more to attract birds and butterflies. Chachalacas stop by, attracted by a neighbor's trees growing grapefruit and oranges.

He decided to enter as a landowner and photographer because, "I wanted to be able to keep both shares of prizes and I wanted to be able to photograph whenever I had the chance," he said.

He photographed from February to June, many times from the comfort of his bedroom window. "I could be watching television while I waited for something to go through," he said. At night he would go out with a flashlight to find nocturnal creatures, such as katydids and spiders.

The Mission-born, self-taught photographer has had his work appear in such books as *The Big Click*, photo essays of Texans enjoying the 1993 Fourth of July. He entered Brownsville's Gladys Porter Zoo photo contest in the 1990s and had his work in its annual calendar.

Luciano takes Jordan, his 12-year-old daughter, to Bentsen State Park every Saturday to foster a love of nature and photography. She won Fourth Grand Prize in the Youth Division II.

"I just like being outside," she said, peering at her father's slides. "I learned how to use a camera, and about different animals."

"And it's a nice way to spend time with her dad," added Luciano's wife, Vicki.

Luciano anticipates planting more native vegetation in his yard. "I'd like to put in a couple of Mesquite trees and a patch of Prickly Pear Cactus that would bloom and make good background," he said, "and maybe some Turk's Cap to attract hummingbirds, and a small pond."

-Jennifer C. Smith

Buff-bellied Hummingbird

FIRST PLACE, Birds
BEST OF CONTEST
PEOPLE'S CHOICE

The Buff-bellied Hummingbird is a marvelous flier. Hummingbirds are the only birds that can fly backward, a necessity when backing out of a tubular flower after nectaring. "Buff-bellies" can be seen collecting spider webs from cactus for building their tiny nests.

Nikon F3 with 180mm f2.5 lens; Fuji Provia 100

Fifth Grand Prize

Photographer: Lynn Bieber-Weir

Landowners: Allen & Kellie Williams
Williams Wildscapes

The lush pine trees and the bald eagles in Lynn Bieber-Weir's yard back in British Columbia are a far cry from the cactus and Buff-bellied Hummingbirds of the Rio Grande Valley, but the contrast only makes her appreciate the Valley's natural diversity. "I will always have a fondness for this very special brushland," she said. Lynn moved back to British Columbia in May 2004 after 13 years in the Valley.

When she won fifth place in the Small Tract Competition, it was her photos of a thrasher and dragonfly that captured the judges' attention. "I'm thrilled," she said.

Lynn photographed at Allen and Kellie Williams' property from February to May. She balanced photography with her nursing job at Rio Grande Regional Hospital in McAllen. "I had a very understanding boss who allowed me to work with rubber boots and camo gear," she said, laughing.

Working on Williams' land was a different experience for Lynn, who also entered as a photographer in 2000 and 2002, a time when she became accustomed to navigating ranchland.

The Williams' two-and-a-half acres in the middle of Pharr, Texas, have drawn more than 2,700 visitors since October 2002 questing after the many rare birds that have appeared there. The 48 species of trees and shrubs and 20 species of ground cover entice a surprising number and variety of wildlife. Allen Williams observed, "I wanted to have it as my own little neat place to birdwatch. I didn't realize it would turn into a good example of a diverse habitat."

Williams' land and family offered perks for their visiting photographer. The three small boys of Allen and his wife, Kellie, became fascinated by her spider slides. "The kids' reaction was absolutely phenomenal," she said. "They wanted to know the names of everything and where I found these things."

"It's so wonderful to see a couple bringing up kids to appreciate the environment," she added. "The kids' natural enthusiasm that came out of this was priceless."

Lynn has been a photographer since the age of 10. "I'm a serious amateur, because I earn my keep by being a nurse," she said. But nature photography continues to tug at her heartstrings. She said she enjoys "the absolute wonder of being out in the South Texas brushland. It's just you and nature."

"Man has made changes in it, but he can't really tame it," she said. "There is so much to see and so much to examine and the light changes everything. I love the cactus."

–*Jennifer C. Smith*

Roseate Skimmer

THIRD PLACE, Insects

Dragonflies are often found basking in the warm sunlight, resting before their next flight to search for food such as mosquitoes. The most evolved of fliers, the dragonfly can fly upside down and backward, and do rolls and loops.

Canon EOS 3 with 500 mm f4 IS lens; 1/250 sec at f5.6; Kodak E100VS

Curved-billed Thrasher

SECOND PLACE, Birds

Often found scratching in the leaf litter under shady bushes, the Curve-billed Thrasher is a bird of the Southwest and South Texas. Thrashers are excellent mimics and their repertoire can include hundreds of sounds.

Canon EOS 3 with 500 mm f4 IS lens; 1/125 sec at f5.6; Fuji Provia 100

White-tailed Deer

SECOND PLACE, Mammals

The White-tailed Deer fawn is both curious and cautious as it silently moves about the brush country. These young deer lose their white spotted pattern within their first year, as it is no longer needed for camouflage when they hide in the deep grass.

Photographer: Annette Word
Landowner: Eutiquio M. Elizondo and Ana M. Guzmán, La Serena Ranch

Nikon F5 with 80-400mm VR lens; 1/125 sec at f4.5 ; Fuji Provia 100

Green Anole

THIRD PLACE, Reptiles and Amphibians

The Green Anole is comfortable around people and can be rather curious. This lizard is sometimes confused with true chameleons as it can change color hues from its normal green to brown, gray or reddish brown.

Photographer: Ariel P. King
Landowners: Ariel P. King and George Powell

Canon EOS Elan II with 100-400mm lens; 1/45 sec at f5.6; Fuji Provia 100

Green Anole

FIRST PLACE, Special Categories

The sights of nature can be beautiful as well as unusual, such as the outline of a Green Anole from behind a Sabal Palm frond. Anoles are seen basking in the sunlight between meals of insects, spiders and other arthropods.

Photographer: Bill Leidner
Landowner: Frontera Audubon

Gulf Coast Toad

SECOND PLACE, Reptiles & Amphibians

A fairly common toad found in most habitats in South Texas, including irrigation ditches and storm sewers, the Gulf Coast Toad has a rather flat appearance. This toad can be identified by the dark stripe down its side and the deep V shape between its eyes. Its glands release a strong irritant that serves as a defense against predators.

Photographer: Gina Rivera
Landowner: Francisco and Gina Rivera

Canon Rebel 2000 with 100mm Macro AF lens; 1/125 sec at f5.6;
Fuji Provia 100

Katydids can come in various shapes. They might resemble leaves to hide from predators. Katydids are actually more similar to crickets than to their family, the grasshoppers. They received the name from their unique sound.

Katydid
FIRST PLACE, Insects & Arachnids

Photographer: Kevin J. Hurt
Landowner: Celia & Luis Perez, 2H-Dos Hermanos Ranch

Canon EOS 5 with 180mm f3.5 L lens; Fuji Sensia 100

Youth Photo Contest

Youth photographers from South Texas and as far away as Maine and North Carolina competed in two age groups: Division I – 16 to19 years old and Division II – 11 to15 years old. Allowed to photograph anywhere in the eight counties of South Texas, except zoos, their quest was to photograph and submit up to five 35mm slides in each of five divisions: Birds, Mammals, Insects & Arachnids, Reptiles & Amphibians and Special Categories, including Action, Animal Babies, Camouflage, Humor, Landscape/Waterscape, Patterns, and Sunrise/Sunset.

Three well-known local judges individually scored the submissions, awarding points to each image, with bonus points given to those images selected for the top three places in each division. The highest over-all point recipients were designated Grand Prize Winners.

Winners shared $2,500 in cash awards, and the Youth Division I Grand Prize Winner was awarded a trip for himself and a parent to the 2005 North American Nature Photography Association's annual summit in Charlotte, North Carolina. There he had the opportunity to meet, learn from and gather inspiration from the best in the industry.

–*Bob Simpson*

Youth Photo Contest
PORTFOLIOS

Youth Photo Contest
Division I (16-19 years old)

First Grand Prize

Photographer: John W. Kastelein

Jumping Spider

FIRST PLACE, Insects & Arachnids
BEST OF CONTEST

Great to have in gardens, spiders rid plants of harmful insects, making them a natural alternative to pesticides. The Jumping Spider is a fast predator and often tackles insects much bigger than itself, using its excellent vision to track down its prey.

Canon EOS 1V with MPE 1-5x 60mm macro lens; Fuji Provia 100

The facial disk of the Barn Owl enables it to locate mice at night by focusing sounds on its ears on each side of its face, allowing it to hear in stereo. The Barn Owl will often use hunting blinds as its roost and nest spot, as large trees with cavities are becoming scarce.

Nikon F100 with 200mm macro lens; 1/125 sec at f8; Fuji Velvia 50

Barn Owl
FIRST PLACE, Birds

Texas Horned Lizard

FIRST PLACE, Reptiles & Amphibians

Home to a vast array of reptiles, the South Texas brush country hosts the threatened Texas Horned Lizard. Long a favorite pet of youngsters throughout the region, the "horny toad," as it is also known, is rapidly declining because of pesticide poisoning of its main food source, the Red Harvester Ant.

Nikon F100 with 200mm macro lens; 1/125 sec at f11; Fuji Provia 100

Green Lynx Spider

SECOND PLACE, Insects

Colorful as the flowers where it hunts, the Green Lynx Spider is a common spider in South Texas wildflower patches. Not a web builder, the Green Lynx chases down prey in vegetation and often catches pollinators that come to flowers.

Nikon F100 with 200mm macro lens; 1/250 sec at f11; Fuji Provia 100

Western Diamondback Rattlesnake

SECOND PLACE, Reptiles & Amphibians

With a growth potential of seven feet, a loud rattle, strong poison and a known tendency to stand its ground, the Western Diamondback Rattlesnake has earned its fierce reputation. Found in many dry habitats, its diet consists of rabbits, rats, mice and ground squirrels.

Nikon F100 with 14mm rectilinear lens; 1/125 sec at f22; Fuji Provia 100

Honey Bee

FIRST PLACE, Special Categories

The wildflowers of South Texas put on a marvelous show in mid-spring, especially along ranch and country roads. Besides water, pollinators such as the Honey Bee are an important part of flower production.

Nikon F100 with 200mm macro lens; 1/250 sec at f11; Fuji Provia 100

Second Grand Prize

Photographer: R.J. Sindelar

Audubon's Oriole

SECOND PLACE, Birds

Named after famed ornithologist James Audubon, the Audubon's Oriole is a striking bird. Its sweet melodious calls and song are a sure way of locating this bird, which is often hidden in thickets along riparian habitats in the western parts of the Rio Grande Valley.

Canon EOS 3 with 300mm lens and 2x teleconverter at f8; Fuji Velvia 100

Rio Grande Leopard Frog

THIRD PLACE, Reptiles & Amphibians

One of the most common amphibians in South Texas, the Rio Grande Leopard Frog can take on several different shades of color from green to light brown, and its pattern can be variable as well. The leopard frog is helpful in controlling insects in any body of standing water.

Canon EOS 3 with 300mm lens and 2x teleconverter at f8; Fuji Velvia 100

Giant Swallowtail

THIRD PLACE, Insects & Arachnids

South Texas is a butterfly haven, and mid-fall is the best time to observe the most species. The Giant Swallowtail is the largest and most common of the several species of swallowtails in the area. Citrus and citrus-like native plants serve as food.

Canon EOS 3 with 300mm lens and 2x teleconverter at f8; Fuji Velvia 100

Curved-billed Thrasher

THIRD PLACE, Birds

The Curve-billed Thrasher is one of those special birds only found in a few places in the United States. Many nature tourists travel to South Texas to catch a glimpse of this often secretive bird.

Canon EOS 3 with 300mm lens and 2x teleconverter at f8; Fuji Velvia 100

Black-bellied Whistling-Duck
SECOND PLACE, Special Categories

There are those special moments in nature when all is well, and life is as beautiful as the scene in which it plays out. A quiet country pond is a wonderful spot to find a mother Black-bellied Whistling-Duck and her large clutch of young.

Photographer: R.J. Sindelar

Canon EOS 3 with 300mm lens and 2x teleconverter at f8; Fuji Velvia 100

Third Grand Prize
Photographer : Gabrielle Salazar

Eastern Cottontail
SECOND PLACE, Mammals

Taking safety in the darkness of evening, the Eastern Cottontail rabbit makes a meal out of windmill grass. If the cottontail's white fluffy tail is not visible, one can look at the rounded tips of its ears to distinguish it from a jackrabbit, whose ear tips are pointed and tipped in black.

Nikon F5 with 170-500 mm f4.5-5.6 lens; Fuji Provia 100

Green Anole

THIRD PLACE, Special Categories

Camouflage is the name of the game if you are the favorite food of another animal. The Green Anole, though rather brave around humans, has perfected hide-and-seek by changing colors from green to brown.

Nikon F5 with 70-180 mm lens; Fuji Provia 100

Fourth Grand Prize

Photographer: Joseph Delesantro

The Corsican Sheep is a hybrid sheep and looks much like the Dall's Sheep of Alaska and Northwest Canada and the Bighorn Sheep of West Texas. Many introduced game species can be found on South Texas Ranches.

Canon Elan II with 500mm f4.5 lens; Fuji Sensia 100

Corsican Sheep

FIRST PLACE, Mammals

Fifth Grand Prize

Photographer: Schuyler Moore

Great Horned Owl

HONORABLE MENTION, Birds

The largest of North America's owls, the Great Horned Owl is a master hunter of mice, small snakes and other animals. The "horns" on its head are neither ears nor horns, but actual feathers that it can raise or lay down smooth. These headpieces work great as camouflage, blending in with the tree branches.

Sunset

HONORABLE MENTION, Special Categories

Day's end nears as the sun sets over a country pond lined by native brush. The colorful hues of the sky reflect off the life-giving water as animals are drawn to the pond for one last drink.

Mexican Ground Squirrel

THIRD PLACE, Mammals

Water is the most important factor of life for South Texas wildlife, and the watering hole is often visited by many otherwise leery species. The Mexican Ground Squirrel, with its rows of white squarish spots, is a common visitor and a joy to see.

Photographer: Jessica Quintanilla

Canon Rebel 2000 with 100-400mm, Fuji Provia 100

Youth Photo Contest
Division II (11-15 years old)

First Grand Prize
Photographer: Allan Delesantro

Long-billed Curlew
FIRST PLACE, Birds

Found in shallow water or on grassy fields, the Long-billed Curlew is obviously named for its bill. The curlew winters in South Texas, feeding on insects and similar fare.

Canon Elan II E with 500mm f4.5 lens; Fuji Sensia 100

Black-bellied Whistling-Duck
THIRD PLACE, Birds

Once rare in South Texas, the Black-bellied Whistling-Duck is now found in many areas and often nests in urban settings where it can find tall trees with cavities in which to lay its eggs. The Tree Duck, as it was once known, is a most colorful and beautiful duck with sharp color contrasts.

Canon Elan II E with 500mm f4.5 lens; Fuji Sensia 100

Green Lynx Spider

SECOND PLACE, Insects & Arachnids

One of the most vividly colored spiders in South Texas is the Green Lynx Spider, which leaps from flower to flower catching its prey with great agility and precision.

Canon Elan II E with 180mm f3.5 L macro lens; Fuji Sensia 100

Black-tailed Jackrabbit

FIRST PLACE, Mammals

Ears flopping as it speeds across open grasslands, the Black-tailed Jackrabbit is fast and agile. More prone to take flight than hide, the jackrabbit depends on speed to outrun its foes.

Canon Elan II E with 500mm f4.5 lens; Fuji Sensia 100

Barn Owl

FIRST PLACE, Special Categories

Barn Owls typically lay five to ten eggs, but when food is scarce they lay fewer eggs or may not breed at all. Babies are vulnerable until they learn to fly. Before they fledge their only defense is to hiss, scream and grunt, while swaying back and forth to show their bravado.

Canon Elan II E with 180mm f3.5 macro lens; Fuji Sensia 100

Grasshopper

FIRST PLACE, Insects & Arachnids
BEST OF CONTEST

Grasshoppers are an important part of the food chain, being a favorite prey of birds, rodents and reptiles.

Canon Elan II E with Canon 180mm f3.5 L macro lens; Fuji Sensia 100

Mexican Milksnake

THIRD PLACE, Reptiles & Amphibians

Often mistaken for the poisonous but similarly colored Texas Coral Snake, the Mexican Milksnake is non-poisonous and offers no threat to humans. Remember the old rhyme, "Red on black, friend of Jack; red on yellow, kill a fellow!"

Canon Elan II E and 28-135mm lens; Fuji Sensia 100

Rio Grande Leopard Frog

SECOND PLACE, Reptiles & Amphibians

Rather small for frog standards, the Rio Grande Leopard Frog is only two to three inches in length. It is highly adaptable to arid conditions and breeds when rain falls. Listen for its short guttural trills during the wet season.

Canon Elan II E with 180mm f3.5 macro lens; Fuji Sensia 100

Mexican Ground Squirrel

THIRD PLACE, Mammals

Comical yet serious, the Mexican Ground Squirrel surveys its surroundings from its burrow hole and doesn't stray far from safety. It often lives in colonies in sandy or gravelly soil, where its burrows are flush with the ground.

Canon Elan II E with 500mm f4.5 lens; Fuji Sensia 100

Bordered Patch

THIRD PLACE, Insects & Arachnids

One stunning butterfly is the Bordered Patch, with its yellow and gold hues. It lays eggs exclusively on the Cowpen Daisy, and the eggs in turn hatch into caterpillars that feed on the same plant.

Canon Elan II E with 180mm f3.5 macro lens; Fuji Sensia 100

Gulf Coast Toad

FIRST PLACE, Reptiles & Amphibians

Found along the Gulf Coast from Mississippi to Costa Rica, the Gulf Coast Toad is rightly named, but it does range inland quite extensively. Its call is likened to that of a wood rattle.

Photographer: Allan Delesantro

Canon Elan II E with 28-135mm lens; Fuji Sensia 100

Second Grand Prize

Photographer: Antonio Vindell

Coyote

SECOND PLACE, Mammals

The most adaptive, cunning, brave and hardy of all mammals in South Texas is the Coyote. A canine, "Ol' Wiley" Coyote spends hot days in underground dens and is more active at night.

Third Grand Prize
Photographer: Danielle R. DeLeon

Laughing Gull
SECOND PLACE, Birds

The most common gull along the Gulf Coast is aptly named for its raucous, laughing call. The Laughing Gull ventures inland during the summer months but is mostly found along beaches, where it might look for a handout from a beachgoer.

Canon Rebel with 35-80mm lens

Fourth Grand Prize
Photographer: Jordan E. Guerra

Giant Swallowtail
HONORABLE MENTION, Insects & Arachnids

The Giant Swallowtail flutters with slow determined wing beats as it goes from one nectar source to the next. Named for its swallow-like tail protrusions and for its size, the Giant Swallowtail can sometimes be found with missing tails, having narrowly escaped being a bird's dinner.

Nikon F6 with 200 mm f4 lens; Fuji Provia 100

Great Kiskadee

HONORABLE MENTION, Special Categories

Inquisitive and bold, much like its colorful plumage, the Great Kiskadee is often found in populated areas and backyards. Photographers could only dream of having their own picture taken by the animal subject at hand!

Photographer: Jordan E. Guerra

Nikon F6 with 200 mm f4 lens; Fuji Provia 100

Fifth Grand Prize
Photographer: Ian M. Gibson

Orbweaver

HONORABLE MENTION, Insects & Arachnids

Known for its expertly woven spherical webs, the Orbweaver is a master at catching insects using webs often stretched over large areas. Orbweavers are usually colorful species with long legs and impressive shapes.

Canon EOS 650 with EF20-210mm lens; Kodak Ektachrome 200

Killdeer

SECOND PLACE, Special Categories

Nature's mechanisms for survival are truly amazing, as can be seen in so many species' behavior. The Killdeer feigns a broken wing and runs across open ground to draw predators away from its nest, which is built right on the gravelly ground.

Photographer: Kaitlin E. Labus

Canon EOS 650 with EF70-120mm lens and 2x teleconverter; Kodak Ektachrome 200

Wildflowers

THIRD PLACE, Special Categories

Spring has truly arrived when South Texas fields are covered in wildflowers. Bluebonnets and Gallardias can be found along most stretches of highways.

Canon EOS 650 with EF70-120mm lens and 2x teleconverter; Kodak Ektachrome 200

Small Tract Competition and Youth Photo Contest Judges

Photo by Laura Elaine Moore

Steve Bentsen
Nature Photographer / Veterinarian
McAllen, TX

One of the founders of The Valley Land Fund, Steve Bentsen has been a professional nature photographer for over 30 years. His work has been widely published in many state, national and international publications. Today he continues to pursue his twin careers of veterinary medicine and freelance nature photography/writing. He has entered numerous VLF competitions, always placing in the top 10. He was The Valley Land Fund's Circle of Life award recipient in 1997.

Photo by Paul Denman

Larry Ditto
Nature Photographer
McAllen, TX

Larry Ditto has been engaged in nature photography for nearly 30 years. During most of that time he worked as a refuge manager in the National Wildlife Refuge System, including Santa Ana/Lower Rio Grande Valley National Wildlife Refuges. After retiring in 1999, he became a full-time professional photographer and partnered with Greg Lasley of Austin to win First Grand Prize in The Valley Land Fund's 2000 South Texas Shootout. Larry placed 3rd and 4th, respectively, in the 2002 and 2004 Shootouts. His work appears in numerous publications and he was The Valley Land Fund's Circle of Life award recipient in 2004.

Photo by Larry Ditto

Lance Krueger
Wildlife Photographer and Outdoor Writer
Mission, TX

Lance Krueger is a full-time professional photographer and outdoor writer with a BBA in Marketing from the University of Texas-Pan American. He travels extensively across the United States and Canada in pursuit of game species with his camera and is considered one of the top deer photographers in the U.S. As an active member of the Outdoor Writers' Association of America, his images have appeared in magazines, books, catalogs, calendars, brochures, advertisements, websites, artist paintings, apparel, and even on billboards. His photos have also won prizes in various national photography contests.

Someday we may look back and realize that man has preserved and enhanced those parts of nature deemed to have economic value and discarded those viewed as having none.

–*John F. Martin*

ACKNOWLEDGMENTS

Sponsors

Our Sponsors are the cornerstone of the Wildlife Photo Contests. Landowners and photographers are able to build upon the solid foundation our Sponsors provide. Generous funding by these individuals and businesses makes our conservation work possible. They reflect our community's conscience in support of the work that The Valley Land Fund does. Please let them know that you appreciate their involvement. Without them, there would be no contest.

Special Acknowledgment

The Valley Land Fund especially recognizes and offers our gratitude
to the Valley Chevy Dealers Association, Chevy Suburban,
GMAC and the Nature Conservancy for their continued
joint support of the South Texas Shootout.

South Texas Shootout

OFFICIAL

Official Airport - McAllen Miller International Airport

Official Vehicle – Chevy Suburban

FIRST GRAND PRIZE

The Vannie Cook Award

Texas State Bank

Boggus Motors

Rhodes Enterprises, Inc.

South Texas Health System

SECOND GRAND PRIZE

The Argyle & Margaret McAllen Award

McAllen Ranch Properties

Wells Fargo

THIRD GRAND PRIZE

The Coneway Family Foundation

Guerra Brothers Successors Ltd.

Frost National Bank

FOURTH GRAND PRIZE

Loring Cook Foundation

Blockbuster Video

CopyZone

Inter National Bank

Mayfair Properties

Little Caesar's Pizza

NAI Rioco Realty

FIFTH GRAND PRIZE

Magic Valley Electric Co-op

DIVISION

Alamo Bank of Texas

AEP / Central Power & Light

Forest Oil Corporation

Johnson Brothers Construction

Shepard Walton King Insurance Group

CLASS

Russell & Jeannie Barron

Boultinghouse Simpson Architects

Britton's Photo Imaging

Jones & Cook Stationers

Martin Farm & Ranch

McAllen National Bank

Palace Cleaners

Payne Auto Group

Photo Craft Laboratories

Rio Valley Electric

Schaleben Limited Partnership

John K. Walters, Jr.

RARE CAT AWARD

Carol Rausch

Bill & Susie Robertson

Frank Smith Toyota

D. Wilson Construction Co.

DIGITAL COMPETITION

AEP / Central Power & Light

CopyZone

Freedom Communications

Gateway Printing & Office Supplies

The Brownsville Herald

Mid-Valley Town Crier

The Monitor

Valley Morning Star

ADDITIONAL SUPPORT

Advantage Rent-A-Car

Bill Burns

Casa Santa Ana

El Rocío Retreat Center

Dr. John Gerling

KRGV TV Channel 5

L & F Distributors

Los Ebanos Preserve

Office Furniture U.S.A.

Pérez Ranch

James A. Person, DDS

RGV Outdoors Center, Inc.

Rio Grande Valley Harley, Inc.

Texas Produce Association

Sponsors

Small Tract Competition

GRAND PRIZE
Doctors Hospital at Renaissance
Humana Insurance
Lee's Pharmacy
Rio Grande Regional Hospital
Valley Baptist Medical Center

DIVISION
K & E Investments
Pete & Vicki Moore
Valley Insurance Services

ADDITIONAL SUPPORT
Clampitt Paper Company
Corso Farms
Georgia Mason Memorial

Youth Photo Contest

GRAND PRIZE
The Robert L. Townsend Award
Star of Texas Energy Services

DIVISION
H.E.B.
Loring Cook Foundation
Blockbuster Video, CopyZone,
Inter National Bank, Mayfair Properties,
Little Caesar's Pizza, NAI Rioco Realty

ADDITIONAL SUPPORT
Abraham Technologies, Inc.
Hunt's Photo & Video

*Sponsor
of the year*

CHARLES CLARK CHEVROLET CO.

Kirk Clark has served The Valley Land Fund
for many years as volunteer, Board member,
Master of Ceremonies, sponsor of programs
and events and all-around leader.

We are honored to name
Charles Clark Chevrolet Co.
as Sponsor of the Year.

*The Clark family and our associates at Clark Chevrolet, McAllen,
have been delighted to support and work with The Valley Land Fund
to acquire, conserve and protect critical wildlife habitat in South Texas.*

*We are hopeful that our shared efforts will add to the quality of life
for all citizens of South Texas, as well as the critters.
We are delighted to be part of The Valley Land Fund legacy.*

Thank you.

*Spirit engaged,
Kirk Clark, President*

Photographers

To be a successful wildlife photographer requires time, patience, knowledge and pure grit. These photographers accepted the challenge of a "wildlife treasure hunt" and produced the outstanding images in this book.

South Texas Shootout

Ken C. Allaman
Hamilton, TX

Barbara Baird
Galena, IL

Ken Beard
Spring, TX

Richard L. Beeckman
Saginaw, MI

Ted Bragg
Granite Shoals, TX

Bill Burns
McAllen, TX

Bill M. Campbell, MD
Oak Ridge, TN

Arnoldo Cantú, Jr.
Alamo, TX

David Cantú
San Juan, TX

Gary C. Carlton
Virginia Beach, VA

Bill Caskey
Austin, TX

Don R. Dean
Houston, TX

Michael Delesantro
Weslaco, TX

Paul Denman
McAllen, TX

Vern Denman
McAllen, TX

Larry Ditto
McAllen, TX

Mary Donahue
Harlingen, TX

Bill Draker
Bandera, TX

Randall Ennis
McAllen, TX

Dennis Erhart
Santa Fe, NM

Catherine Evans
Tomball, TX

William Ewing
McAllen, TX

Rafa Flores
McAllen, TX

Alta Forshage
McAllen, TX

Eddie Forshage
McAllen, TX

Omar García
Austin, TX

Cynthia Guerra
Mission, TX

Roel Guerra
Mission, TX

Beto Gutierrez
Edinburg, TX

Derrick Hamrick
Raleigh, NC

Rex Hewitt
Laguna Vista, TX

Irene Hinke-Sacilotto
Joppa, MD

Joseph Holman
Brownsville, TX

Lowell Hudsonpillar
Mission, TX

Mary Jo Bogatto Janovsky
Harlingen, TX

Kermit Denver Laird
Starkville, MS

John C. Livas
Houston, TX

Sonny Manley
Missouri City, TX

Gary McHale
Richmond Hill, ON

Carlos A. Nuñez
Brownsville, TX

Rolf Nussbaumer
Live Oak, TX

John Pickles
Barataria, LA

Brendan C. Quigley
New York, NY

Roel Ramírez
Roma, TX

Jimmy Smith
Richmond, TX

Tom Urban
Falfurrias, TX

Larry L. Von Behren
St. Louis, MO

Nancy C. Von Behren
St. Louis, MO

Sharon R. Waite
Mission, TX

Jeremy Woodhouse
McKinney, TX

Tony C. Worley
McAllen, TX

Ken York
Mission, TX

Photographers

Small Tract Competition

Guillermo Aguilar
San Benito, TX

Lynn Bieber-Weir
McAllen, TX

Taylor Blanton
San Benito, TX

Lynn Brezosky
Harlingen, TX

Robin Bullard
McAllen, TX

Robert Cantú
McAllen, TX

Edgar Castro
Mission, TX

Esperanza S. Chapa
McAllen, TX

Joe Corso
McAllen, TX

Tony Corso
McAllen, TX

Carla M. Ellard
San Marcos, TX

Jackie Field, Jr.
McAllen, TX

E. Andrea Garcia
Harlingen, TX

Ruben Garcia
Edinburg, TX

David C. Garza
Brownsville, TX

Diane M. Garza
Brownsville, TX

Juan L. Garza
Harlingen, TX

David Gelfer
Brownsville, TX

Luciano E. Guerra
Mission, TX

Michael R. Hannisian
Mission, TX

J.D. Hensz
McAllen, TX

James Brian Hersey
Victoria, TX

Suzanne Herzing
Mission, TX

Shawn Horton
Alamo, TX

Kevin J. Hurt
Edinburg, TX

Amy Johnson
McAllen, TX

Kenneth Johnson
McAllen, TX

Ariel P. King
Mission, TX

Joseph Labus
Edinburg, TX

Bill Leidner
Mission, TX

Miguel Angel López
Rio Grande City, TX

Miguel S. López
Rio Grande City, TX

Adan Maldonado
Edinburg, TX

Mike McKinney
Olmito, TX

Jo Ann Mitchell
McAllen, TX

Maricella Molina
Edinburg, TX

Daniel A. Montelongo
Reynosa, Tam., Mexico

Wallace G. Prukop
San Benito, TX

Patty Raney
Harlingen, TX

Gina Rivera
Mission, TX

Stephen Rene Rogers
Edinburg, TX

Sally Ross
Mercedes, TX

Victor E. Sanchez
McAllen, TX

Cindy Sigrist
Mercedes, TX

John Sigrist
Mercedes, TX

Steve Sinclair
Brownsville, TX

Elias Smith
New York, NY

Rob Stevenson
McAllen, TX

Susan Stevenson
McAllen, TX

Debra Thomas
Edinburg, TX

Tony Vindell
Brownsville, TX

Ester R. Volpe
McAllen, TX

Martin S. Volpe
McAllen, TX

Cara E. Wade
South Padre Island, TX

Thomas Henry Watkins
San Benito, TX

Annette Word
McAllen, TX

Photographers

Youth Contest Division I

Stephanie Chavez
McAllen, TX

Joseph Delesantro
Weslaco, TX

Brian Denman
McAllen, TX

Leslie Dyke
McAllen, TX

Tyler Elliff
Harlingen, TX

Patty Guerra
Mission, TX

Erin M. Holland
Mission, TX

Katie Holland
Mission, TX

John W. Kastelein
Bristol, ME

Erin Keelin
Port Isabel, TX

Stephen Leidner
Mission, TX

Max Magee
Edinburg, TX

Schuyler Moore
San Benito, TX

Jessica Quintanilla
McAllen, TX

Isidoro Ramirez, Jr.
Harlingen, TX

Analisa Rodriguez
Brownsville, TX

William A. Rolando
San Isidro, TX

Gabrielle Salazar
Pleasant Garden, NC

R.J. Sindelar
Houston, TX

Youth Contest Division II

Elliott Canales
La Joya, TX

Hunter Englebert Cofoid
McAllen, TX

Joshua Corso
McAllen, TX

Tiffany Leigh Cowart
San Isidro, TX

Danielle R. DeLeon
Mission, TX

Allan Delesantro
Weslaco, TX

Jazmin Elizondo
La Joya, TX

Frank Allen Ferris, Jr.
Harlingen, TX

Carl D. Flowers II
Mission, TX

Ian M. Gibson
McAllen, TX

Jordan E. Guerra
Mission, TX

Lauraly C. Hernandez
Weslaco, TX

Mariel Hernandez
La Joya, TX

Jessica Klement
Mission, TX

Kaitlin E. Labus
Edinburg, TX

Wendy Medina
Mission, TX

Kelsi Nelson
Mission, TX

Mary Frances Noell
Progreso Lakes, TX

Marco A. Pérez
San Juan, TX

Kristi Saba
McAllen, TX

Joanna Schiefelbein
Mission, TX

Jillian Sigrist
Mercedes, TX

Kaylee Ayn Turner
San Benito, TX

Bertha Vasquez
La Joya, TX

Juan Pablo Vielma
Pharr, TX

Antonio Vindell
Brownsville, TX

Ricky Walker
McAllen, TX

Ryan Walker
McAllen, TX

Joseph Whitacre
McAllen, TX

Landowners

Private landowners play a crucial role in the conservation of wildlife and habitat. Without their efforts entire ecosystems may be lost to future generations. We appreciate them allowing us to venture "Beyond the Ranch Gate".

South Texas Shootout

William R. Buchholz

Buena Vista Ranch

Bill Burns Ranch

A. Cantú Farms

Cap Rock Pens

Colima Ranch
Michael Scaief
and Charles Kennedy

Las Colmenas Ranch
Margaret and Robert McAllen

The Cozad Ranch

El Devisadero Ranch
Miguel A. and Analicia Q. García

Dos Rios Ranch
Arroyo Colorado

Newt and Maggie Dyer

Falfurrias Cattle Co, Inc.

Flores Ranch

Glory Ranch
Herb and Nancy Scurlock

Bobby and Leslie Guerra

Guerra Brothers Ranch

Hacienda La Esperanza
Garcia Land and Livestock

Douglas Hardie Ranch

Inn at Chachalaca Bend
Cleve and Rosemary Breedlove

King Ranch, Inc.

La Brisa Ranch
Larry and Betty Lou Sheerin

La Mota Ranch
South Texas Nature Retreat

Las Majadas Ranch
Winifred R. Wetegrove

John and Audrey Martin

Metz and Waite Farm
Sharon R. Waite

Payne Ranch

Ramírez Ranch
Roel Ramírez

RGV Outdoors Center
Mary Jo Bogatto Janovsky

Rio Grande Container Game Ranch
Mark Gibbs and Harold Jones

San Pedro Ranch
Baldo Jr. and Daniel Vela

Santa Cecilia Ranch
and Rancho Margo La Coma

Frank Schuster Farms
Frank Schuster and Becky Jones

Skipper Ranch
Daniel L. and Tricia Drefke

Speer Ranch
Darrell and Suzie Thompson

Starr Feedyards, Inc.

El Tecolote Ranch
Phil and Karen Hunke

Tecomate Ranch Partners

Varal Ranches, Ltd.

Weaver Ranch
Ken and Barbara Weaver
Kent and G'Anne Weaver

H. Yturria Ranch

Roberto and Fran Yzaguirre

Landowners

Small Tract Competition

2H - Dos Hermanos Ranch
Celia and Luis Pérez

Cielo Escondido
James and Georgina Matz

Corso Farms

Charles J. Ellard

El Monte del Rancho Viejo
Mr. and Mrs. David C. Garza

El Montecito
Amy and Kenneth Johnson

El Rancho de las Retamas

El Rocío Retreat Center
Marsha Gamel-Nelson

Jackie and Trudy Field, Jr.

Frontera Audubon

Luciano E. Guerra

Los Ebanos Preserve
Martha Russell Blanton

Indian Ridge Bed and Breakfast

Barbara Kennett

Ariel P. King and George Powell

La Serena Ranch
Eutiquio M. Elizondo, Jr.
and Ana M. Guzmán

Joseph Labus

Llano Grande Country Club

Lawrence V. Lof

Miguel Serna López

Mike McKinney

Wallace and Judi Prukop

Rancho Chachalaca
John and Audrey Martin

Rancho El Javeline
Shawn W. Horton

Rancho Lomitas
Benito and Toni Treviño

C.L. and Patty Raney

Resaca Grove Farms

Rio Viejo
J.D. Hensz

Francisco and Gina Rivera

Ross Family

Sklarz Farms Ptn.
Jim and Larry Skloss

Southern Fields Aloe, Inc.

Valley Nature Center

Volpe Homestead
Ester R. and Martin S. Volpe

Tony and Sharon Vindell

Williams Wildscapes
Allen and Kellie Williams

Book Patrons

Since our first book from the 1994 Contest, we have relied on Book Patrons to cover the cost of production. Patrons agree to buy a minimum of 20 books - early on, sight unseen. This financial vote of confidence allows us to have the book essentially paid for before we hit the print button.

250 or more books
Rio Grande Regional Hospital

100 or more
A.G. Edwards & Sons, Dennis Burleson, Greg Douglas,
    Bill Martin & Pat McClellan
Chase Bank of Texas
Cook Ranches
Corrigan Benefits, Bob & Susan Corrigan
Gateway Printing & Office Supply, Inc.
Knapp Medical Center
South Texas Health System

50 or more
Children's Dental Center, Phil & Karen Hunke
CopyZone
First Community Bank
Graves, Dougherty, Hearon & Moody
Hollon Oil Company, Bill & Cynthia Hollon
Inn at Chachalaca Bend
Kittleman, Thomas, Ramirez & Gonzales, PLLC
McAllen Chamber of Commerce
Shepard Walton King Insurance Group
Texas State Bank - McAllen

40 or more
Alamo Bank of Texas
Boggus Ford
Charles Clark Chevrolet
Kirk & Jeri Clark
Guerra Brothers Successors Ltd.
In Touch With Nature - Barbara Baird, Photographer
Jones & Cook Stationers
Lee's Pharmacy & Medical Equipment Co.
Rolf & Karen Nussbaumer
Rhodes Enterprises, Inc.
Texas State Bank - Harlingen

Troy Giles Realty
Weyerhaeuser

30 or more
Descon Construction, LP, Mickey C. Smith
Johnson Brothers Construction
La Joya ISD, Instructional Resources
Lynne Tate Real Estate
John & Audrey Martin
The Prudent Investor, Johnny & Susan Johnson
Sokolosky-Sullivan Financial Team

20 or more
Patrick H. Admire, CPA
Am-Mex Products, Inc.
Apple Construction & Development, Inc.
Katharine Armstrong
Artline America Inc. & Masterpiece Café
Averill Builders, Joe and Nancy Averill
Ballenger Construction
Mr. & Mrs. Lee Bass
Bert Ogden Rio Grande Valley
Martha & Taylor Blanton and John & Judy McClung
Boultinghouse Simpson Architects
Broadway Hardware & Gifts
Brownsville Convention & Visitor's Bureau
Buena Vista Ranch
Burns Ranch
Gift Honoring Bill L. Burns, Burns Ranch
Burton Companies
Burton, McCumber & Cortez, LLP
Hazel Burrows
Cactus Flower Gifts & Interiors
Cage Ranch
El Clavo Lumber Company, Inc.
The Cozad Ranch
Country Casuals

Closner Equipment Co., Bennett & Susan Closner
Jean Cress
Cupco Utility & Paving Co.
Rip Davenport & Associates
Davis Equity Realty
Dizdar Development
Dyer & Associates, J.W. Dyer
Echo Hotel & Conference Center
Edinburg Chamber of Commerce
Edwards Abstract and Title Co.
Dr. & Mrs. E.M. Elizondo, Jr.
Ellis, Koeneke & Ramirez, LLP
Engvall & Hlanvinka, LLP
Dr. Michael & Mrs. Ruth Evans
First National Bank - Edinburg
Foremost Paving
Friends of Laguna Atascosa National Wildlife Refuge
Friends of Santa Ana National Wildlife Refuge
Frontera Produce Ltd.
Frost Bank
Dr. Jeffrey Glassberg & Dr. Jane Scott
Law Office of Ricardo R. Godinez
Greater Mission Chamber of Commerce
Guthrie's Locksmith & Safe
Mr. & Mrs. H.B. Hause
Kenneth M. & Carla C. Haynes
Helle's Fine Furnishings, Mary Helle
Jim & Karen Henderson
Hidalgo County Historical Society
Colleen Hook
Larry T. & Mary Jane Hunter
Images for Conservation Fund
IMS Home Health Care, Inc.
Indian Ridge Bed & Breakfast
Inter National Bank
Iwo Jima Museum & Gift Shop
Law Offices of Glenn Jarvis

Book Patrons

Kellogg Chevrolet - Honda
Nana Kendall
Charles Kennedy
Ariel P. King & Friends
Knapp Chevrolet
Kolder, Inc.
The Rollins M. & Amalie L. Koppel Foundation
Kreidler Funeral Home, Inc.
Las Colmenas Ranch, Margaret & Robert McAllen
Las Majadas Ranch, Winifred R. Wetegrove
Marion R. Lawler, Jr., MD
Brian & Laura Lewis
Lifetime Industries, Inc.
Lone Star National Bank
Long Chilton, LLP of McAllen
Long Chilton, LLP of Brownsville
Magic Valley Electric Cooperative
The Man's Shop
Martin Farm & Ranch Supply Inc.
Howard I. Mason & Millicent Bleakney Mason
City of McAllen
McAllen Construction, Inc.
McAllen Economic Development Corporation
Lowry & Jessica McAllen
McAllen Miller International Airport
McAllen National Bank
McAllen Ranch Properties
McMullen County Title Co.
Melden & Hunt, Inc.
David Merrill
Mike's Loading Service
Dr. Charles F. Mild, Interventional Cardiology
Mission Nursing Home
The Monitor
Pat & Beverly Moody
Pete & Vicki Moore
Mother Nature's Creations
Pat Moyer
Naturally Curious, Inc.
Nuevo Santander Gallery
Office Furniture, USA
Oh Kay's!

Stacy L. Owen
Payne Auto Group
Joe & Shawn Patterson
Dee Ann Pederson - Windows of Nature by Dee Ann
Buck & Penny Pettitt
Pharr Chamber of Commerce
Photo Craft Imaging
John & Lica Pinkston
Professional Appraisal Services, Inc., John & Dottie Malcom
Quips 'n' Quotes
The Law Offices of Thomas G. Rayfield
Carol Rausch
Re/Max in the Valley, Eva Jean Radle
Renee's of Sharyland, Renee Martin & Tomas Tijerina
Rex Hewitt Photography
Rio Bank
Rio Grande Container Game Ranch, Mark Gibbs
      & Harold Jones, Owners
Bill & Susie Robertson
Rowland Enterprises, Inc.
Joe Lee Rubio
Russell Plantation
El Sacramonte Ranch, Dr. & Mrs. George J. Toland, Jr.
Salinas, Allen & Schmitt, LLP
Santa Cecilia Ranch, Jorge & Dilia Pérez
Schaleben Limited Partnership
Dr. Frank & Helen Shepard
Dr. Steve & Suzanne Shepard
Mrs. Wayne Showers
Sierra Title of Cameron & Willacy Counties
Silverbrook Ranches
R.J., Rick & Patti Sindelar
South Padre Island Chamber of Commerce
Southern Texas Title Company
Trev & Donna Jo Sparks
Speer Ranch
Spence Concrete, Co.
Starr Feedyards, Inc.
Bill Stocker & Orvis Akers
Stone Brothers
Larry & Ellen Stone
TexNEP

Texas Cooperative Extension - Nature Tourism Program
Molly Thornberry
Tipotex Chevrolet, Inc.
The University of Texas - Pan American
The University of Texas - Pan American Foundation
Valley International Airport
Valley Nature Center
Van Burkleo Ford - Mercedes
Van Burkleo Motors - McAllen
George & Claire Vaughan
Paul G. Veale, Jr.
Walker & Twenhafel, LLP
Betty & Roscoe Watkins
Wells Fargo
Sheldon & Eve Weisfeld
Linda Williams
Willms Engineering & Surveying Co.
Sandra Sweeney Wilson
H. Yturria Land & Cattle
Yturria Ranch
Roberto & Fran Yzaguirre
Roger A. Zessin, A.G. Edwards & Sons

Book Patron Committee

Brian Lewis, Chair
Kirk Clark
Jean Cress
Robert Dunkin, II
Alice East
Somer East
Amy Johnson
Audrey G. Martin
David Merrill
Myra Pérez
David Rowland
Beth Zambrano

Visions of South Texas Contributors

COMMITTEE

Audrey Gluck Martin, Editor
Jan Epton Seale, Copy Editor
Lowry McAllen, Contributing Editor
Clare Bercot
David Cantú
Carolyn Ennis
Mark Gibbs
Ariel King
John Martin
Jessica McAllen
Judy McClung
Bob Simpson
Beth Zambrano

CAPTIONS & TECHNICAL

Martin Hagne
Selena and Ken King
Lisa Williams
F.P. (Tony) Bennett

DESIGN & LAYOUT

Esperanza S. Chapa
Tony Corso, CopyZone

PRINT COORDINATION & COLOR

Blue Fusion Design, Bob Carter

PRINTER

Gateway Printing & Office Supply, Inc.
Lin Miller

STAFF

Myra Pérez
Beth Zambrano

WRITERS

Clare Bercot is a long-time Valley resident and a tax partner with Burton McCumber & Cortez, LLP. She serves on several boards, including the Brownsville Botanical Gardens and Arboretum. Her spare time is devoted to nature, the arts and spending time with her daughter.

Mark Gibbs is co-owner of the Rio Grande Container Co. and Game Ranch. The ranch won First Grand Prize in the 2002 Wildlife Photo Contest. Mark is an avid outdoorsman who spends every weekend hunting or fishing. Born in Houston, Texas, Mark has made the Rio Grande Valley his paradise for the past eight years.

Martin Hagne is Executive Director of the Valley Nature Center in Weslaco, Texas. He sits on several nature-related boards, leads nature field trips, and volunteers for environmental and wildlife entities. Birding, nature viewing, and an interest in native plants of the Valley are great passions.

Audrey Gluck Martin is a founding Valley Land Fund board member and wife of Photo Contest originator, John F. Martin. A retired financial planner, Audrey seeks to add economic value to wildlife and habitat through photography. She and John live on their private wildlife refuge near Edinburg.

Lowry McAllen was born and raised in the Rio Grande Valley. He manages his family's ranch land in northwest Hidalgo County, where he lives with his wife, Jessica. He has worked as a writer in Mexico, Guatemala and the state of New Mexico.

Richard Moore is a South Texas native and president of Valley Nature Films LLC. He is a professional wildlife videographer and writer. He hosts a popular television program and also produces a weekly page, "Outdoors with Richard Moore" for the Valley's three major dailies.

Jan Epton Seale is a McAllen writer and writing teacher and has helped edit previous Photo Contest books. Jan enjoys studying and writing about the Valley's special flora and fauna. A recent book, co-authored with her photographer son Ansen Seale, is *Valley Ark*, a photo-poetry volume featuring Valley wildlife.

Bob Simpson is an architect and partner in the firm of Boultinghouse Simpson Architects. A Valley native, Bob served two years as President of the VLF and has been a photographer participant in three Photo Contests. His wife Lita and three teenage daughters indulge his favorite outdoor activities such as fly-fishing, hunting, wildlife photography, and birdwatching.

Jennifer C. Smith is the environment, science and health reporter at *The Monitor* newspaper in McAllen, Texas. A native New Yorker, she graduated from New York University with a bachelor's degree in journalism and history.

Beth Zambrano is Programs Director for The Valley Land Fund and a part-time instructor for South Texas College. She and husband Luis moved to the Rio Grande Valley in 1996 with their newborn daughter. She enjoys travel and being outdoors, while keeping track of her son in college.

The Valley Land Fund
Wildlife Photo Books

Visions of South Texas: Beyond the Ranch Gate is the sixth book
to be produced from the Wildlife Photo Contests.
These books educate and inspire.

Treasures of South Texas (1995)   *Focus on the Wild* (2001)

Creatures on the Edge (1997)   *Spirit of the Chaparral* (2003)

The Lens and the Land (1999)   *Visions of South Texas* (2005)

More than a Photo Contest

For almost 20 years a dedicated group of volunteers has been working toward a vision: that of our children, grandchildren and future generations enjoying the same awe-inspiring outdoors that we knew as children. We understand that protecting the unique South Texas ecosystem, the habitat and wildlife that calls the southern tip of Texas home, is crucial. We also understand that the future of wildlife habitat is, for the most part, in the hands of private landowners.

By creating the Wildlife Photo Contests we've given landowners an additional opportunity for raising awareness about the value of responsible land stewardship. We've assisted them in exploring other avenues for preserving, protecting, and sometimes re-creating valuable wildlife habitat. Nature tourism and photo blind leasing are, in part, offshoots of The Valley Land Fund's philosophy that there needs to be economic value in protecting wildlife habitat.

More than a photo contest or a book, the VLF is a non-profit land trust, working to protect land with a variety of conservation tools. When most people think of "protected" land they think of the national and state parks, and other government-owned refuges. These are wonderful places; but approximately 94% of land in Texas remains in private hands. Land trusts work with landowners to find the optimum method of protecting and preserving their land, and with families who want to create lasting legacies of land ownership.

Since 1986, The Valley Land Fund has permanently protected nearly 7,000 acres of ranchland by accepting conservation easements – agreements that limit or prohibit development and ensure wildlife habitat and green space protection. Landowners give up certain rights and the land trust commits to monitor the property in perpetuity to ensure that the grantors' wishes are carried out.

The Valley Land Fund also owns outright and provides stewardship to some 50 acres of property that are notably valuable wildlife sites.

The "protection" business in Rio Grande Valley ecology circles is cooperative, not competitive. Proceeds from the Wildlife Photo Contests and other fundraising efforts have been used to assist in the purchase of land, which was later conveyed to entities such as Texas Parks and Wildlife Department, U.S. Fish and Wildlife Service, the City of Harlingen and the City of McAllen. Partnerships with other conservation groups include The Nature Conservancy and Frontera Audubon.

The future of South Texas is a little wilder thanks to the foresight and hard work of The Valley Land Fund. We encourage you to become more involved. Join us as we work to raise public awareness of the unique South Texas landscape and its wildlife needs. Help us prevent the beautiful book you hold in your hand from becoming a mere history book about what *once* existed in the Magic Valley of South Texas.

–Beth Zambrano

2004 Board of Directors and Staff

Mission Statement

To preserve, expand and enhance the native wildlife habitat in the Rio Grande Valley through education, land ownership and creation of economic incentives for preservation.

OFFICERS
Bob Simpson, President
Judy McClung, VP - Photo Contest
Pat Moody, Treasurer
Somer East, Secretary
Cleve Breedlove, Past President

MEMBERS
Joe Averill
Lynn Bieber-Weir
Rosemary Breedlove
Christine Yturria Buford
Bill Burns
David Cantú
Tony Corso
Larry Ditto
Robert Dunkin, II
Bill Elliott
Rafa Flores
Oscar García
Amy Johnson
Neal King
Wes Kittleman
Brian Lewis
Audrey G. Martin
Virginia Meyer
Jorge Pérez
David Rowland
Jack Scoggins, Jr.
Wayne Showers

Randy Sweeten
Danny Vela
Eryn Wingert
Allen Williams
Fran Yzaguirre

ADVISORY BOARD
Martha Russell Blanton
Taylor Blanton
Dennis Burleson
Kirk Clark
Alice G.K.K. East
Evelyn East
A.R. (Felo) Guerra
Dr. Marla Guerra
Carla Haynes
Karen Hunke
Dr. Phil Hunke
Jane Kittleman
John Martin
Jan Seale
Ron Smith
Billy Snider
Lynne Tate

HONORARY BOARD
Joe Charles Ballenger
Dr. Steve Bentsen
Carol Rausch
Dr. Don Farst

Mark Feldman
Dr. Juliet García
Jack Hart
Kevin Hiles
Bill Hollon
Tom Koeneke
James A. McAllen
T. Edward Mercer
Pete Moore
Dr. Gary M. Schwarz
Frank Yturria

STAFF
Ruth Hoyt, 2004 Photo Contest Director
Beth Zambrano, Programs Director
Belle Cedillo
Merritt Hunke Kennedy
Myra Pérez

THE VALLEY LAND FUND

2400 North 10th Street, Suite A
McAllen, TX 78501
(956) 971-8550
www.valleylandfund.com

Afterword

Are you feeling, at the close of this book, an almost out-of-body experience? A trip to some other world triggered by the presence of these images of wildlife up close and personal?

To observe animals going about their lives, in an existence that we are ineffably barred from knowing, brings longing, humility, and finally, love. It's not the love of valentines, but the kind of passion we might feel for the stars, the wind, or our beautiful blue-shrouded earthball seen from space.

The word *animal* came from the Latin *animalis* meaning *living*. *Animalis*, in turn, emerged from an even older meaning, *soul*. This etymology does not necessitate theological pronouncements on whether animals have souls. Each of us keeps our private opinion, depending on what we may have fathomed, completely apart from science, in the eyes of a deer, a snake, or a beloved pet.

Rather it is for us to note the presence of the animals as a deeply sacred trust. They are here for reasons ever unknowable. To relegate their existence to a total rationalism is ultimately a sad commentary on human hubris.

It is enough that our every action and reaction toward the animals emanate from a spirit of thanksgiving. Our efforts acknowledge our never-ending delight at being permitted existence in a world blessed with these mysterious beings. We observe one wonderful beast after another and say, "Yes. Thanks be."

To live with love in the midst of this "soul" kingdom is to claim our spirit's stance, our true human domain.

–Jan Epton Seale

INDEX

Index

Index

Index

—Index by Clare Bercot